Faith for Fiery Trials: Vol. IV

From the Valley to Victory with Mountain-Moving Faith

The following translations have been used:

Scripture quotations marked KJV are from the King James Version of the Bible.

Scripture taken from the New Century Version®. Copyright © 2005 by Thomas Nelson. Used by permission. All rights reserved.

Scripture quotations marked NKJV are from the New King James Version of the Bible. Copyright © 1979, 1980, 1982 by Thomas Nelson, Inc., publishers. Used by permission.

Scripture quotations marked NIV are from the Holy Bible, New International Version ® NIV®. Copyright © 1973, 1978, 1984 by International Bible Society. Used by permission of Zondervan Publishing House. All rights reserved.

Scripture quotations marked NLT are from the Holy Bible: New Living Translation. 2004. Illinois: Tyndale House Publishers.

Scripture quotations marked (TLB) are taken from The Living Bible, copyright © 1971 by Tyndale House Foundation. Used by permission of Tyndale House Publishers, Carol Stream, Illinois, 60188. All rights reserved.

Ordering Information
Quantity sales and special discounts are available on quantity purchases by corporations, associations, and others. Please email at **contact@nicolesmason.com**.

Printed in USA

Faith For Fiery Trials: Volume IV: From the Valley to Victory With Mountain Moving Faith
ISBN: 978-1-7347912-5-9

In Loving Memory of:

Ebone´ Wilson
March 3, 1992 – March 3, 1992
Angel Baby of Pastors Willie & Mary Wilson

Dedications

Priscilla Ademola

This book is dedicated first to God who gave me the strength to write my story.

Secondly, to my husband, Thompson Ademola, who always supports me and believes in me.

I also want to dedicate this book to my beautiful children who are a blessing to me.

I also want to dedicate this book to my mother, Jolanda Groos Jones, who made so many sacrifices for me and my sister to have a better life in the Netherlands.

Finally to my spiritual mother and mentor, Nicole Mason, whom I met in 2015 at a conference in the Netherlands. I want to thank her for her love, encouragement, counsel, and prayers.

Trashawna Carter

This is dedicated to Trashawna Carter for the courage to release her life testament through a transparent light in order to heal and help others! What a journey. No more shame. I just want to thank you, Lord. NOW HERE!

To those who knew my story, I thank you from the bottom of my heart for your continued belief, encouragement, pushing, love, support, patience, and especially understanding.

Special thanks to my husband, Mark; my children, Michael, Malcolm, Markus, and Tatayanna; my sister Tyra; my uncle Phillip; and my tight sista circle.

Michelle Clark

This chapter is dedicated to my late mother, Carolyn Patricia Clark. A woman who specialized in telling people the hard truth with love. My grandma, Naomi Gross Clark; I understood her love language at a very young age, and she believed in me even as a child.

Dr. Aikyna Finch

I would like to thank everyone who supported and encouraged me during my ministerial journey. Over the years, God blessed me with some great people who saw past me being a woman and saw the potential in me. Each one played a different role in making me the minister I am and will become; so, thank you so much for your presence, guidance, and love!

Minister Da´Mali Goings

To my parents, who always believed in me;
To my friends, who have supported me through thick and thin;
And to my readers, who have made this all possible;

Thank you for being a part of my journey.

This book is dedicated to you and the many women who have experienced life challenges. Lose it all to gain the one in you.

Elaine Harris

I would like to thank my husband, Henry, for his love and support. I don't know what I would do without him. My son Jason and daughter Brittany, who have always stood by my side in caring for Devin; you are my village that I can always depend on. I do not know what I would do without you. Thank you, and I love you all.

I would also like to dedicate this book to my father, Ralph G. Harper, who passed away in 2018. You were always there with your love and support, providing me with words of encouragement, and pushing me to be the best that I could be. I only wish you were still here to see my recent accomplishments. You are missed beyond measure; we love you, Daddy.

Deborah Johnson

First, I would like to thank God for this opportunity to share my story. I'd like to also thank Dr. Nicole Mason for her encouragement, the push to become greater, and for allowing me to participate in this 4th Volume of Faith for Fiery Trials.

To my family: my dad, Bishop Weldon Johnson; twin brother, Darryus Johnson; and sister, Margie Johnson; your love and support are unwavering. I'm grateful for the authentic bond we have. I love you forever and always! To my daughter, Brooke Elena Johnson, and my son, Jayden Eric Johnson, my heartbeats; you both are the reason I keep going. I will always be your number-one cheerleader. You are my everything, and I love you both forever and always.

To my mentor - Dr. Vikki Johnson. Thank you for your guidance, mentorship, and sisterhood during some of the most challenging times of my life. I appreciate you and the Soul Wealth tribe.

Finally, to my mom, Jacqueline R. Johnson, who gained her wings on December 16, 2020. My life has forever changed, but I'm thankful for what she has instilled in me. Even though she is greatly missed, I promise to make her proud!

LaShaune Lee

Jesus – My Savior, my King, my Friend that truly sticks closer to me than anybody. To the One who really knows me—the good, bad, and ugly about me—and decides *every day* to love me and choose me! MY HEART BELONGS COMPLETELY TO YOU! I LOVE YOU!

Shelton – My 'Ride or Die,' my bestie, the one that matches my crazy. I love you with my whole heart. Thanks for being my #1 fan, my support system, and my 'wallet.' Lol! It's our time, baby; let's do this!!! I love you!

Andre, Chris, and Branden – My heartbeats. You are my gifts, my reasons to smile. You make life worth living. You are my 'whys' and my legacy. I know I can be a lot sometimes, but mostly I hope I make you proud. I love you!

My Parents – Ma, thank you for being my 'she-ro.' Every time life knocked you down, you got back up! I learned so much from you—I still do. Thank you for always having my back and never letting me go. Dad, thanks for doing your best. I know it was not always easy, and life was unfair at times. You did not give up, and I am grateful. I love you both!

Bishop and Co-Pastor Owens – You are the greatest pastors in the whole world! God knew I would need you, and He gave me His best! I am the servant leader that I am because of your examples. I love you both!

Elder Nicole Mason – Girrllll. Lol! Thank you for chasing me down and having patience with me. Because of your obedience to God, I am walking into a new realm that I did not think was possible for me. Bless you. I love you!

To my Girls – Everything I survived was for you. I am called to you. You have changed me forever. I am grateful. I LOVE YOU ALL!

Chaplain Paulette McPherson

I thank my Lord and Saviour, Jesus Christ, for His goodness and mercy; I would be nothing without Him.

I dedicate this book to the memory of my parents, John and Dorenda Cummings, and my son Nathan James McPherson, who have gone on to be with the Lord.

To my children Chantelle and Jonathan; I love you more than all the stars in the sky, and I am uber proud to be called your 'mommy' and 'mama.'

To my small circle of girlfriends who have stood by me (UK & USA), thank you for our years of laughter, tears, and prayers. Thank you for holding my arms up and believing in me during the rough and challenging times. I love you, ladies.

To Bishop Alfred A. Owens, Jr., who first declared that I would be an author in 2016; thank you for your wisdom, being my spiritual father, and always being at the end of an email or text.

To Nicole S. Mason, Esq; I didn't see this coming! Thank you for believing in me, pushing me, and our God-ordained friendship.

1 Corinthians 2:9 (New King James Version): "[9] But as it is written: 'Eye has not seen, nor ear heard, Nor have entered into the heart of man The things which God has prepared for those who love Him.'"

Tracy Morgan

First, I would like to thank and honor my amazing husband Keith for his support and encouragement during this process. He works along with me as my radio producer, and it is a joy. Your love and support have given me the courage to pursue my dreams and embrace my passions. Thank you for all that you do. I love you.

To my daughter Katrina. You are such an inspiration to me. I dedicate this chapter to you. I pray you truly understand you are loved more than I could ever express.

To my mom. You always remind me that I can do anything. Your unwavering love and belief in me has given me the courage I need. Thank you for always supporting me through my good ideas and even the bad ideas.

Finally, to my dad and dear friend Doreen. Although they are no longer with us, I know they would be so proud of me. Knowing this brings me much joy and comfort.

Katrina V. Perry

I dedicate my second published work to God and my village. My parents, Howard and Viola Cary, who I pray would be godly proud of me. My children and grandchildren, who are my heartbeat. My bonus parents, siblings, and bonus siblings who love me unconditionally and support all my efforts. My friends who provide counsel, make me accountable, and give me a safe space to just be. I thank God for this amazing opportunity through Elder Nicole Mason. This and all my future work will be for your glory, Lord!

Dr. KeyShaze Ward

I dedicate this chapter to my Lord and Savior, who has empowered me to share my testimony with the world so that others will come to know Him and be free. Secondly, I dedicate this book to the strong women on whose shoulders I stand: my mother, my grandmothers, and countless mentors who saw greatness in me before I did. Thank you! Lastly, to all who can't seem to dig out from the pain of their past; rise up, face the pain, and become who God has designed you to be!

Rev. Mary L. Wilson

I give all glory and honor to God for keeping me and guiding me.

I honor and dedicate my words to my parents, Mary and James Lewis, who laid the foundation for my life's work.

To my family who have patiently and lovingly been the wind beneath my wings.
My husband, Rev. Willie F. Wilson, who is my constant companion, number-one encourager, and 'iron' that keeps MY iron sharp.

Lastly, Elder Dr. Nicole Mason ... Thank you for seeing the God in me and showing your LOVE in ACTION!

Indea Webb

To my Lord and Savior Jesus Christ who loves me and gave Himself for me. To the beautiful, fearless women of courage, faith, strength, wisdom, virtue, and prayer that came before me: Minnie, Violet, Alice, Arentha, Ethel, Dorothy, Della, Everlene, Trula Ann, Eula, and Precious. Because of them, I AM! In loving memory of my great grand aunt Sarah who is my mirror. To all the women who have felt 'unpretty,' I pray that you find your inner beauty that is fearfully and wonderfully made. A beauty that was knitted together within your mother's womb. To all my friends and relatives. Thank you for your patience during my journey. My final and most immeasurable gratitude goes to my mom, the wind beneath my wings! Thank you for all the sacrifices you made. The prayers. The love. The support. The drying of tears. The discipline. The advice. The laughter. The joy. The birthing. Love you more!

CONTENTS

Introduction

The old adage is true, "Never judge a book by its cover." This statement rings true for the women of this edition of the *Faith for Fiery Trials* Franchise. *Faith for Fiery Trials: Vol. IV: From the Valley to Victory with Mountain-Moving Faith* is a powerful testament to the Scripture found in Isaiah 43:2 (New International Version NIV), "When you pass through the waters, I will be with you; and when you pass through the rivers, they will not sweep over you. When you walk through the fire, you will not be burned; the flames will not set you ablaze."

These women DO NOT look like they've come close to drowning or that they were in the midst of a burning, hot fire; they don't even smell like smoke. I would even venture to say that looking at them and reading their stories will almost leave you scratching your head because the two just don't add up. Or do they? God is the great equalizer in our lives. He can bring high mountains that seem overwhelming down. He can part rivers that surely will drown you and cause His people to walk over on dry ground. He can cause a fiery furnace to be a mere 'walk-in closet' that allows room for movement but becomes miraculously fire-resistant. This is the God that you will encounter in this book.

Let me warn you: the stories are raw, revealing, and saturated with the anointing of a powerful God to bring healing, hope, and help to your own deep dark secrets, hurts, and pain. You did not purchase this book, pick this book, or digitally download a copy by accident. You are on a collision path with a mighty God who is in love with you, wants the best for you, is calling you higher, and has more in store for you because He has need of YOU! Yes, YOU!

I know you may have been told that you will not be able to rise above what has happened to you. But the devil lied to you; that family member lied to you; that significant other lied to you. You may have even internalized the lie and continually rehearse it to yourself. These women serve as proof that you can rise above your greatest challenge because they did it.

The Bible says in Acts 10:34, (King James Version KJV) "…God is no respecter of persons." What He has done for one, He can do for you too! Open your heart, breathe deeply, and expect God to minister to you through the experiences of the women who have been sent to speak to you for a time such as this!

Beauty for Ashes
Indea Webb

To all who mourn in Israel, He will give a crown of beauty for ashes, a joyous blessing instead of mourning, festive praise instead of despair. In their righteousness, they will be like great oaks that the LORD has planted for His own glory. —Isaiah 61:3 (New Living Translation NLT)

This is *my* testimony. I am a survivor of emotional, physical, spiritual, and verbal abuse. My journey toward healing has been long, but I pray that sharing my story will bring you closer to finding your own healing. I will admit that I was filled with anxiety about sharing my story. *What would people think of me? Who do you think you are?* I asked myself. Well, I am a fighter who refuses to be defined by her trauma. I am a fighter who fought back against the weight of isolation, secrecy, and self-blame. I have reclaimed *my* sense of personal power. I have reclaimed *my* voice.

The testimony I am about to share is my own lived experience. It contains descriptions of emotional and physical violence that may be triggering. Please consider your own triggers and well-being in reading. It is important for me to tell my testimony because it has helped me heal my hidden pain and advocate for others caught up in the trap of darkness and shame. You see, the devil did not want me to be born. A few months before I entered the world, my mom decided to visit her older sister, my aunt, who lived in a two-story townhouse. At the end of the visit, my mom suddenly fell down the stairs in the house. She was terrified of a miscarriage but thankfully kept me inside her womb. Eventually, the day of my birth arrived at a hospital of the Catholic faith. On a Thursday. This was ironic because there is a phrase that states, "*Thursday's child has far to go.*" Oh, if I only knew. Baldhead, wide-eyed, and chubby-cheeked, I was a joy to my parents and family. I was a quiet baby, which proved to be symbolic throughout my life. My mom said that I was not fussy and allowed her a whole night's rest. Something she immensely enjoyed as a new mom.

I was a photogenic baby, and at one point, my mom considered moving to New York for me to be chosen for a Johnson & Johnson baby advertisement. However, she changed her mind. She had safety concerns about living in a big city. New York was off the table. So, we stayed in the Midwest, and at the age of nine months, my parents divorced. It was an event that would greatly impact me emotionally throughout my youth and into adulthood. Divorce is painful, but the impact upon children is even greater than people and families realize. For example, negative feelings toward one parent can be unconsciously inflicted upon the child or children by members of a family. For me, it led to feelings of abandonment as I grew older.

The months went by, and when I was around one year old, my mom was involved in a car accident while driving her Volkswagen Beetle. The impact of the crash was on the driver's side; I was in the backseat, strapped into a car seat. According to my mom, the force of the hit was so powerful that I could have been propelled out of the vehicle. Again, the devil did not want me to live. It appeared he was relentless in attempting to kill me.

As with all babies, it was time to learn to walk, talk, and reach all the other important milestones. One unexpected shift was when I was two, and my mom moved to Dallas, Texas. At that young age, I'm not sure I had a concept of physical beauty, even though I developed a fascination with the Dallas Cowboys Cheerleaders, so much so that I aspired to grow up and become one. I loved everything about them: the cowboy hat, white fringed and sparkling blue vest, star-studded belt, and white boots. I mean, what was there not to like? My fascination with the cheerleaders did not override the fact that my mom wrapped me in a lot of love. She was my place of comfort, encouragement, and safety. Even at a young age, she allowed me to be 'Indea.' Little did I know that this would be challenged later in life.

Dallas was a temporary residence, and my mom moved back to the Midwest. Kindergarten came, and my mom enrolled me in a Catholic school where I learned my ABCs and 123s. I thrived and was promoted to first grade, where my life changed. I was subjected to an educational nightmare. Trauma. My teacher labeled me as being learning disabled. My mom, a teacher by profession, knew something was wrong. Thankfully, she had a close friend who was finishing a Ph.D. in Special Education. Mom's friend completed a series of tests and determined that I needed eyeglasses based on my eye movement. As a result, she recommended a local ophthalmologist who substantiated that I needed eyeglasses. With eyeglasses in tow, my mom disenrolled me from Catholic school. She enrolled me in the public school system, where I excelled academically, thanks to two black women who knew this young black girl was not learning disabled.

However, it was not long before the taunts came. With my new eyeglasses, I was teased mercilessly and often called 'four-eyes' or had fingers placed into my face with the question "How many fingers am I holding up?" I was quiet (like a baby) and took it in stride, but deep down inside, I was hurt. Then, the summer I turned nine years old arrived. This was an important age because it marked my entrance into adolescence or the pre-teen years. It was a time of beginning to experience significant physical, emotional, and social changes. It was a time that led to a pivotal encounter that would change the course of my life. During this particular summer, I spent a week with my aunt and cousin. He and I are four years apart in age. I was the first female grandchild in my mom's family, and he was the first male grandchild. I can tell you; it was a fun week. My aunt taught me how to play tennis. I did the centipede with my cousin, went to vacation Bible school, played outside until dark, and listened to Michael Jackson. One day, my aunt announced she was taking my cousin and me for a picture.

To this day, I still remember the excitement. I wore a blue summer dress with white ruffles and a light blue headband with a small white rose. My hair was styled in a braided side ponytail with a white ball ponytail holder. I wore my eyeglasses. My cousin also wore his eyeglasses. In fact, our eyeglasses looked similar. With a bright smile, I stood next to my cousin. *Cheese!* The flash of the camera was bright but could not dim our happy faces. The faces of children tanned from the summer. We were rays of sunshine. After the prints were completed, my aunt presented copies to my mom.

I took one of the copies, and with joy in my heart, I excitedly showed off the picture among family and friends. I waited for a reaction, and then it came from a male family member, "They made you look like a monster!" I was devastated. People often think of abuse as being only physical, but it can also be verbal and cause emotional harm. According to Safe Horizon, Inc., the nation's most prominent crime victim's agency located in New York, "emotional abuse involves nonphysical behavior that belittles another person and can include insults, put down, verbal threats, or other tactics that make the victim feel threatened, inferior, ashamed or degraded."[1] At nine, I was made to feel ashamed of my outward appearance. Instead of stepping into adolescence with a positive reflection of beauty, I entered with a sense of ugliness. Someone who was supposed to affirm me instead nullified me. I became self-conscious of how I looked and became overwhelmed with a feeling of inferiority. After that statement was made, I pulled out some old photos and realized that I smiled with my mouth closed, which was a sign of my own perceived inward sadness. In my eyes, I was dull, a 'plain Jane,' a four-eyed monster compared to other females I thought were beautiful such as classmates, family, or friends.

---

[1]https://www.safehorizon.org/programs/supporting-someone-emotionally-abusive-relationship/

I believe my mom sensed that inward sadness and strived to affirm me. She encouraged me to always remain true to what God had created me to be. She told me, "You can be 'beautiful' on the outside but 'ugly' on the inside." My grandma Eula, who passed away in 2015, was also a great source of affirmation and inspiration. A sharecropper from Mississippi, she took a dangerous journey in the middle of the night with a child in tow (my aunt mentioned earlier) to join my grandfather in Kansas. If you know anything about the history of Mississippi and the Ku Klux Klan, then you can imagine the danger she faced. She instilled courage, faith, and the love of God in the fabric of her children and grandchildren. It is this foundation that would help bring me out of the ashes.

Years passed, and still, I was ugly in the back of my mind. My identity was distorted because I thought I looked like a monster. Eventually, the emotional abuse I suffered at the age of nine would lead me to a monster of another kind; the kind that almost ended my life at the hands of a man who showered me with platitudes of love but, in reality, engulfed me in pure, unadulterated evil. It seemed that the devil was attempting to end my life again. At the age of 25, I became a victim of dating violence. In all abusive relationships, it's about power and control. It does not start out that way, and my abuser, who was 14 years my senior, began the slow process of love bombing. What is love bombing?

According to Psychology Today, "love bombing is a deliberate and manipulative tactic that is used to gain the upper hand over a new partner through a pattern of overly affectionate behavior such as showering the other person with gifts and/or compliments, declaring love early on, and/or taking steps to remain in constant contact and spend increasing amounts of time together."[2] While it appeared my abuser really 'liked' me, it was a warning sign of an unhealthy relationship. According to the National Domestic Hotline, there are four common examples of love bombing: 'soulmate' status, exaggerated compliments, gifts, and communication overload.[3] Looking back, I can see the 'red' flags.

---

[2]https://www.psychologytoday.com/us/basics/love-bombing
[3]https://www.thehotline.org/resources/signs-of-love-bombing/

My abuser inflicted verbal, emotional, and psychological abuse that eventually turned physical to undermine my self-worth and my identity. The love bombing turned into belittling me and implying that no other man would want me. He tried to isolate me from family members and would become enraged over how I dressed or wore my hair. He would gaslight me and shift blame by saying the abuse was my fault. He was a master manipulator who would terrorize me by saying he would kill my family members if I attempted to end the relationship. I was terrified.

What do I do? I began thinking to myself. My abuser sensed I was attempting to walk away and began increasing the abuse. He yelled and became even more aggressive by calling me 'whore' and 'bitch.' One day, his rage became so intense that he placed a pillow over my face to end my life. Looking into his eyes was like coming face to face with pure evil. I cried out to God, and my abuser suddenly stopped. He apologized and promised that it would never happen again. He pleaded for me not to leave. When his pleas went unheard, he threatened to commit suicide. After months of verbal, emotional, physical, and psychological trauma, I gathered the strength and walked away. I picked up the telephone and contacted local domestic violence organizations for guidance. I knew that I was in a dangerous situation and that my abuser would come back. I looked at my options and developed multiple strategies to gain my freedom and safety.

Victims of domestic violence need a safety plan to optimize their safety, as violence can escalate while attempting to leave. While I could not control my abuser's behavior, I could control my safety. As part of that safety, I obtained a peace order and transitioned to an undisclosed location. However, a piece of paper did not stop my abuser from cyberstalking and attempting to locate me. He never did, but I walked around in fear for years that one day he would. You see, the devil couldn't kill me *physically* through my abuser, but he could paralyze me *mentally* with fear.

Leaving a dangerous relationship was not all sunshine. I did not come out completely undamaged. I was left with scars of post-traumatic stress disorder (PTSD), trust issues, and a minor hearing loss in my left ear that requires me to sometimes read lips or request that a person repeat what they said. I walked around with my head down in shame. I felt like a stick broken into many pieces, a stick with low self-esteem.

I picked up my shame and turned to the church in the hope of it being a place of refuge. I hoped to find emotional, spiritual, and physical support to get on the path toward healing. Instead, I found the opposite. I encountered women who looked at me like I was not fearfully and wonderfully made. They were not aware of my previous emotional and physical abuse, but it was as though they sensed my low self-esteem. What I endured was spiritual abuse. According to *Christianity Today,* "spiritual abuse is a form of emotional and psychological abuse." Yes, let's be real. Congregants can abuse one another. These women, whom I term the 'mean girls,' created a toxic environment that shamed me due to my physical size.

To them, I lacked the essence of being an authentic Black 'woman.' I was not 'curvy' but an Olive Oyl. *What Black woman is an Olive Oyl?* After all the previous trauma I had been through, I was now demeaned with statements such as "Oh, you're so little;" "Look at this little bit;" "How much do you eat?" or the implication, "What man wants a skinny woman?"

I began eating whole cakes and pies, ordered chocolate malts from Potbelly's, and drank high-protein shakes, anything, and everything to gain weight. *Would this make me an 'authentic' black woman?* I wondered. Like Alice in Wonderland, I dropped down a rabbit hole. It was a hole that led to high blood pressure from the emotional trauma and consuming all that unhealthy food. My doctor said that it would lead to serious consequences if I did not get out of that hole. So, I stopped eating the whole cakes and went into isolation. I was mentally tired. Like a car that had run out of fuel, I came to a stop.

Words hurt. The mouth is a mighty weapon that can inflict harm and pain. I sought counseling and spent a lot of time with God. I poured out my anger. My frustration. My guilt. My pain. My tears. My soul. I prayed for those who demeaned me, and I prayed for the strength to forgive. Little by little, I picked up the pieces of my life. I began feeling like sunshine. I smiled more. I laughed more. I started taking back *my* power. My voice. I looked at the devil eyeball to eyeball and said, "Enough is enough. I AM a child of God. YOU are a liar. An imp with NO authority. NO power. YOU ARE DEFEATED! YOU are the UGLY ONE. Not me. Now scram."

The more I stayed close to God, the more I felt His love surrounding me, guiding me on my healing journey. This was never felt more than during the summer of 2021 when I underwent genetic counseling for breast cancer risk. Those results led me to dig deeper into my ancestry DNA. I went through a reputable ancestry service and anxiously waited six weeks for the results. I was astonished by the results, as they provided an ethnic estimate from the Balkan Peninsula of Southeast Europe. *Huh? Balkan*? I thought. Upon closer examination of the map, I noticed it encompassed Thessaloniki, Greece. I found this to be very interesting because Apostle Paul, during his second missionary journey, preached the gospel in Thessalonica for three weeks, where "some of them were won over and joined ranks with Paul and Silas, among them a great many God-fearing Greeks and a considerable number of women from the aristocracy" (Acts 17:4–5, The Message Bible MSG). *Hmm, Aristocratic women. Wow!* I soaked up the results, as it was like reading a story of who I am and my connections with others around the world.

This ancestry journey would continue during the summer of 2022 at my paternal family reunion when I was shown a photo of my great-grandmother and her sister. Looking at my grand great aunt was like looking in a mirror. My physical resemblance to her was uncanny. She was slim. Statuesque. Like me. Even the pose of her arm on the side of her body was like mine. She was Aristocratic— like me. She was beautiful—like me. She was black. Like me. Hallelujah!

Through faith, I survived my fiery trials. It was not easy, and there are days when the memories come flooding back, but the memories no longer cause emotional pain. Instead, I simply say "THANK YOU, Jesus!" because even when I was in the midst of those fiery trials, He was with me. Man may fail you, but God never does. Man may abuse you, but God never does. That's why we can trust Him to get us through the fiery trials and onto the other side of happiness, love, and peace. No longer bound.

I am no longer that nine-year-old girl who thought of herself as an ugly four-eyed monster. I am no longer that 25-year-old woman who found herself in an abusive relationship. I am no longer that woman who thought of herself as an Olive Oyl. All that I endured does not define who I am because family, friends, society, and even church folk will make you feel that you are less than what God has designed you to be. No, I speak against all negativity. Like me, you have to talk to yourself and declare "I will always be at the top, never below" (Deuteronomy 28:13 NIV) and "I am delivered from the power of darkness" (Colossians 1:13 KJV).

Today, I am grateful to be surrounded by women and others who encourage, support, and uplift me. They have helped me to reclaim my voice without judgment. They affirm. They listen. When I look into the mirror, I no longer see a deficient Black woman. I no longer see a woman holding her head down in shame. Instead, I see beauty, strength, and fierceness. I see a phenomenal woman who is a quiet storm with the heart of a lioness.

Through faith, I AM a woman who has risen out of the pain, the tears, the brokenness, and the ugliness that spoke over her. As a result, I AM a woman dedicated to speaking life and not death into other women. I AM a woman devoted to increasing access to justice for victims of domestic violence, stalking, and other forms of gender-based violence. I AM a woman dedicated to dismantling notions of the ideal body type, which is leading women down a dangerous path of cosmetic surgeries such as BBLs, breast augmentations, and other procedures that have led to deadly consequences.

Like the women of Thessalonica, my grand great aunt, and all the women in my familial lineage, I am fearfully and wonderfully made, a woman of nobility wearing her crown of beauty. I am no longer bound by the shackles of low self-esteem. I have reclaimed INDEA. This is *my* testimony, and I no longer find shame in it!

Resources for Victims and Survivors of Domestic Violence

Asian Pacific Institute on Gender-Based Violence (Directory of domestic & gender violence programs serving Asians, Native Hawaiians, and Pacific Islanders, 2023)
https://www.api-gbv.org/resources/directory-api-services/

DeafHope (Deaf DSV Agencies)
https://www.deaf-hope.org/deafagencies/

Esperanza United (Latinas and Latin@ communities)
https://esperanzaunited.org/en/directory-of-national-and-local-organizations/

Jewish Women International (Directory of resources for Jewish survivors and families)
https://www.jwi.org/directory

Love Is Respect (ages 13-26)
1-866-331-9474
TTY 1-866-331-8453
Text: loveis to 22522
Chat Online: **www.loveisrespect.org**
https://www.loveisrespect.org/

Men Stopping Violence
https://menstoppingviolence.org/

Mental Health Services
https://www.nasmhpd.org/content/mental-health-links

National Center for PTSD
https://www.ptsd.va.gov/index.asp

National Deaf Hotline
Videophone: (855) 812-1001
TTY: 800.787.3224
Voice: 800.799.7233
Instant messenger: DeafHotline
Email: **nationaldeafhotline@adwas.org**
https://thedeafhotline.org/

National Domestic Violence Hotline
1-800-799-SAFE (7233)
TTY: 1-800-787-3224
SMS: Text START to 88788
www.ndvh.org

Office on Violence Against Women (OVW) (state domestic
violence and sexual assault coalitions – local resources)
https://www.justice.gov/ovw/local-resources

Pathways to Safety International **(Americans overseas)**
833-SAFE-833
Email: crisis@pathwaystosafety.org
https://pathwaystosafety.org

The Stalking Prevention, Awareness, and Resource Center
(SPARC)
https://www.stalkingawareness.org/

StrongHearts Native Helpline
1-844-7NATIVE (762-8483)
Chat Online: **www.strongheartshelpline.org**

Tahirih Justice Center (Immigrant Survivors)
https://www.tahirih.org/

Techsafety.org (Tech safety resources)
https://www.techsafety.org/blog/2023/3/13/march-2023-new-amp-updated-tech-safety-resources

Ujima – The National Center on Violence Against Women in the Black Community
1-844-77-UJIMA
https://ujimacommunity.org/

U.S. Department of State (International Parental Child Abduction Contacts)
1-888-407-4747 (from the U.S. and Canada)
+ 1 202-501-4444 (from outside the United States)

Questions regarding **preventing** international parental child abductions:
PreventAbduction1@state.gov

For general abduction questions:
AbductionQuestions@state.gov
https://travel.state.gov/content/travel/en/International-Parental-Child-Abduction.html

WomensLaw.org (Restraining Orders)
https://www.womenslaw.org/laws/general/restraining-orders

When God Says Move, M O V E!
Tracy Morgan

I have been blessed to accomplish a lot throughout my career in radio and television. I fell in love with television at the age of 13. I was very passionate and determined to become a television newscaster. However, the road to success wasn't as easy as I imagined.

Thanks to my mother who cooked dinner with the television on, I heard a voice and saw a lovely woman delivering the news one day. Her name was Lark McCarthy. I became obsessed with watching the news every day. I had it bad. It didn't matter what I was doing throughout the day; when it was news hour, everything, and everyone around me had to stop and be quiet. I was determined to be a newscaster just like Lark McCarthy.

One day, I had the opportunity to meet her and interview her for a school project. She was kind and one of the nicest people I have ever met. She doesn't know how nervous I was the first time I spoke with her on the phone. I hung up in disbelief that she took the time to talk to me. This left a lasting impression on me. Years later, I would become that person someone would call to ask questions about my career or to be interviewed for their school project. I always remember how kind Lark was to me. Kindness goes a long way.

Lark was not the only newscaster that had a lasting impression on me. Every summer and sometimes Thanksgiving and Easter, I was sent to California to spend time with my dad's family. While there, I would watch Valerie Coleman, a newscaster on KRON in San Francisco. Like Lark McCarthy, I overcame my nerves one day and called her and asked if I could come to meet her. To my surprise, she said yes. I was so excited. I still remember what I wore. I wore my favorite black blazer, and my hair was fixed in the then-popular 'mushroom' style. I was dressed to impress; they could have easily put me on television that day. You couldn't tell me anything. Just like Lark, Valerie was very nice. She walked me through the studio and introduced me to her colleagues. I was starting to believe that I could become the next famous newscaster.

My journey wasn't easy, but it was blessed. How could it be a rocky ride and a blessed experience simultaneously? God had His hands on my life and career the entire time. I would soon move from middle school to high school, still wanting to be on television as a newscaster. But there was one major setback. I wasn't taking school seriously, which showed up in my grades.

I played sports and was comfortable making the GPA necessary to stay on the team. I was just doing enough to get by. Deep inside, I knew I could do better but chose not to. That was until my English teacher, Ms. Beckmon, got my attention. She caught me walking past her class, talking loud, and using foul language with my friends. I knew I had messed up and immediately apologized to her. My apology was out of fear that she would call my parents and tell them how wild I was acting in the hallways.

Instead of reporting my behavior to my parents, in her very calm voice, she said something that would put me back on track. She said, "I thought you wanted to be a newscaster." That hit me some kind of way. She told me I was failing her class and that I needed English to pursue a career in broadcasting. At that moment, I felt like I had let myself down and my parents, who were very supportive of me. My mom would always encourage me. She believed I could do anything. Her favorite words were "You can do it; just do it." I wouldn't dare tell them about the conversation I had with my teacher. For a minute, I started to believe that maybe I wouldn't become a newscaster, something I had dreamed about since I was 13.

I was told that maybe I should do something with my hands, like become a cashier. I thought perhaps I didn't have what it took to excel in a broadcasting career, but I could still hear my mother's voice telling me I could do it. I would take my teacher's advice and straighten up. I worked hard, and eventually, I was on the honor roll. What a great feeling! Over the years, I have tried to find her to say thank you.

Graduation would soon come. Now that I was focused and mature, I knew exactly what I wanted; to pursue a career in television news. I made the decision not to attend a four-year college but to enroll in the Columbia School of Broadcasting in Virginia. It was the right choice for me, especially since it wasn't long before I had the opportunity to get in front of the camera to do what I dreamed of—working in television news. My first big assignment was covering Reverend Jesse Jackson when he ran for President. I didn't quite know what I was doing, but I was in the room, gathering the story. I had a press pass with my picture on it and felt like I had arrived. I was living my dreams.

I was hungry for my place in the industry. I visited a local television news station in Washington, D.C., that produced The Carol Randolph Show, which featured women on the radio. Here, I met Candy Shannon, one of the smoothest, most talented women in radio. I introduced myself after the show, and she invited me to the radio station. She said that I could always do television but encouraged me to check out radio. One day, I called and asked if I could drop by the station. Candy worked for top-rated WKYS.

The legendary Donnie Simpson and Paul Porter worked at WKYS. When I walked into the studio, I was fascinated and couldn't believe my eyes. Candy sat behind a large control board that she actually operated. When she opened her mouth, she was so smooth, smiling as she introduced the next song. I decided right then that if I could do radio and television, I would. Candy critiqued my tapes until I finally got to a place of applying for jobs. I wanted to be as smooth as she was. To be honest, I longed to sound just like her. I applied to a few stations, and the only one that called me back was an AM gospel station that I was not interested in. Candy told me that if I wanted to be a professional broadcaster, I needed to be able to work in all genres. I was not happy. I wanted to work in R&B radio, but God had other plans for me, and I'm so grateful.

This was the start of my career in radio. I've spent most of my career in gospel radio, and what a journey it has been. It took me some time to realize that gospel radio was no different than any other format. It was a business and my job. The same things that came with other formats happened in gospel radio. I learned early on that I needed to have tough skin if I was going to make it in this industry.

I remember working at a station during a difficult time for me. My dad had just had a stroke and was very ill in the hospital. I was juggling being a wife and a new mom at the time. Work was stressful, demanding, and competitive. I had been working at the radio station for nearly a decade, and I knew my season there was ending. I felt like I had gone as far as I could with them. I was also ready to grow and expand my audience. Every day, it became less desirable to work there. God was directing me to move on; still, I couldn't focus on leaving because I was focused on getting my dad healthy and back on his feet.

My decision not to go only added more stress, but I praise God for His Word that brought me through. I leaned on scriptures like Isaiah 54:17 to get me through, and I spoke healing scriptures over my parents. I must admit I had days of shedding tears, but God would never let me get too down before He gave me the strength to press on. I would reflect on all the times God came through for me. I prayed, fasted, and worshiped. Every day, I showed up to work, opened my microphone, and executed the best show I knew how. The gospel music I played became my encouragement to journey on. I would keep my headphones on and tune everything out or turn up the volume loud enough so everyone in the building could hear it. Every lyric in the songs I played was a blessing to me. The saying is true; sometimes, you have to encourage yourself. God gave me the strength to get through and surrounded me with prayer warriors.

I didn't share much of what I was going through with my colleagues. I just showed up to work, did my job, left, and headed to the hospital to be by my dad's bedside. This was challenging, as I grew further away from the station I once enjoyed working for. I was popular but unfulfilled. A year passed, and I was still there. I learned that it's best to move when God says so. Thank God for His mercy.

It was Christmas Eve. I remember it like it was yesterday. My mom called to share the news that she had just been diagnosed with cancer. I had no idea the seriousness of it. To be honest, I had never heard of colon cancer. She informed me that she was scheduled for surgery in January. At this point, how could I be concerned about leaving my job when my dad's health was steadily declining, and now my mom was diagnosed with cancer?

God has a way of encouraging you, and He did just that. One day, I received a call at work that truly blessed my life. A sweet lady called me to make a song request. I answered the phone, sounding joyful, yet my heart was breaking. I was good at opening the mic and hiding my feelings. Even though I was going through something. I often had to put aside what I was dealing with to encourage someone else, but this day, I needed to be encouraged. I believe this lady was an Angel. Somehow, she knew the joy in my voice wasn't real. She asked me if I was okay. Without asking any other questions, she began to encourage me. She told me to go home and get alone with God. Her exact words were: "You need to cry out to God." The Lord used her to lift me through His Word.

I hung up the phone, amazed at how much God truly loves me. He used a complete stranger to speak life to me when I needed it most. I have no idea who the woman was to this day. She never called back to follow up with me, but I know she was an Angel. You see, my parents were in the hospital the day she called. I took her advice and realized that this was part of the process. God was preparing me for a greater work. I must admit it didn't feel good, but it was necessary for me to get to a place in God to fulfill my purpose.

I remember taking a vacation during this time. It gave me time to stop, think, and regroup. This was exactly what I needed. While on vacation, I decided to make that move to leave the station and step out on faith. God had brought me this far, and I knew He had more for me. I know it was God speaking clearly to me.

Isn't it amazing that your faith jumps to another level when you know it's God speaking to you? I gained the courage I needed. If I wanted to syndicate my radio show and become an entrepreneur, I needed to act and talk like one. I decided to step out on faith. I returned to work, secretly cleaned out my locker, traded my jeans and sweatsuits, and began dressing like a boss. The only things I left in my locker were my headphones. I was ready to submit my two-week notice, but it was a little too late. Two days after cleaning my locker out, when I arrived at work, I was asked to come into the office. The manager told me they had decided to go in a different direction in my position. While this is common in radio, I was disappointed that after bringing the station high ratings, revenue, and popularity, I was not allowed to say goodbye to my listeners, despite my longevity with the company. During the meeting, the manager told me that they would give me time to clean out my locker. That's when it hit me. Wow, God!

I remember smiling and jumping for joy as I left the station. God had already prepared me for that day. My locker was already empty, and I was stepping into my next season. There was no way I could be upset with my former employer for releasing me into my next season. God knew I was taking my time to leave, so He used them to help move me along. Thank You, Jesus! I can say I'm grateful. He had greater waiting for me.

I was blessed to be able to care for my parents while I took a break from radio for a few months. God knew exactly what He was doing. I took all the time I needed to care for them. Unfortunately, my dad passed. However, my mom underwent chemo and has been cancer-free for over 20 years. To that, I say hallelujah. I returned to radio full-time as a morning show host and program director. A short time later, my radio show was picked up and nationally syndicated in over 40 markets. And yes, it's still growing. This journey is a faith walk. We will have tests and trials, but God will never fail us. As the song says, "As I look back over my life, and I think things over, I can truly say that I've been blessed, and I have a testimony."[4] God has been good to me.

Just know that if you've prayed about your situation, and you know in your heart that it is God, don't be afraid to step out on faith. Trust God and move when God says move.

---

[4]https://genius.com/Rev-clay-evans-ive-got-a-testimony-lyrics

Igniting My Power!
Trashawna Carter

We delight in the beauty of the butterfly, but rarely admit the changes it has gone through to achieve that beauty. — Maya Angelou

God aligns time with purpose. You see it in me because it's in you. God called and chose me because it was necessary; I NOW finally see. As a child, you expect that your family will provide a safe environment for you at all times and by any means necessary. How do you manage when your family members are the ones to break that trust through abuse?

Growing up, I always felt like I was THE black sheep of the family that honestly didn't belong because I was teased about being too 'red' or 'yellow.' My lips or my nose were too big. I was considered 'ugly' and too skinny, not to mention who I resembled. You start to believe those things that folks say to you over time. Talk about major self-esteem issues; I had them! The ugly truth that I swept under the 'proverbial' rug for many years was that I was sexually violated repeatedly at the hands of my beloved family members.

Horrific and horrible as that may seem, those were not the most difficult situations. I would literally 'pray' for it to be over with suddenly or that a trusted adult would witness the atrocities and rescue me. What hurt me the most was that I wasn't heard or believed each time I attempted to reach out for help. The truth about some of the abuse came forward only because I became pregnant. I was 16, pregnant by a family member I desperately wanted to be rescued from, and scared with no one to trust. I had always said that if I did not become pregnant, I would have taken all the abuse to my grave.

What's a young girl to do? As you can't successfully hide a pregnancy, I revealed the truth. Man, you know how they teach us to tell a trusted adult; well, that didn't work for me. Because of the hostile reaction I faced, I didn't mention what else I was going through at the pleasure of other family members. I felt there was no point in talking about the abuse since I was considered a liar, 'fast,' and covering up my mistake (becoming pregnant). What young child would say something like this if it wasn't true?

Abortion was my immediate first choice because of how the baby was conceived. When that was no longer an option, I opted for adoption. I was afforded a wonderful opportunity to live in a group home for pregnant girls. I accepted the offer quickly, as I was looking for a safe place to be in peace because I wanted to escape from my so-called 'family.' It was the best choice I could have made for my young self. I was finally at a place where I wasn't being judged. I was actually being accepted. I was living a normal life, except for now being a teen mom with no clue about what I was doing. Ultimately, I decided to keep the baby because I felt the child would love me, no matter what! I thank God for connecting me with people that cared about me and my baby.

Sadly, there seemed to be no change in certain family members' perceptions of me or my situation, even after the court process revealed the truth that I had been telling them all along. The blood test was 99.9% positive that the family member was the father of my baby. This was a devastating hurt. I sought counseling but stopped after a while, as I felt like the counselor and I were not a good fit. I would have kept going if I knew then what I know now.

HEALING!

I thought I was free. However, it wasn't until I started attending church that I learned and understood how bound I truly was. Even with strong biblical teaching, I was not confident in my understanding. I yielded to my ignorance, believing wholeheartedly that I had to get everyone before they got me, showing no mercy. It was me against the world. Unfortunately, this behavior was only detrimental to ME. It caused me to become promiscuous, deceitful, guarded, unforgiving, and suspicious of everyone, especially men.

Nothing is wrong with the things I didn't understand or could not process. How could I? I was still a child. Do I process things better as an adult? Not always. My coping mechanism for years was to sweep things under the rug. So, what changed? I have tripped over that same rug too many times, and now I realize I have no choice but to deal with the actual situation(s).

REVELATION!

Did I forgive those who molested me? Did I forgive family members who didn't protect me? What about those who didn't believe me? These are tough questions because they cause me to reflect on my truths. Let me put it this way, I confronted the person responsible for the pregnancy, and not in a godly manner. This was by far the toughest because of the close family connection. After many years of prayer, I forgave all of the abusers. As for the family members who didn't believe or protect me, I also forgave them. I learned to let the Lord fight my battles. It didn't break me, although it felt like it then. It gave me the strength and courage to FORGIVE and become transparent to help someone else.

How are you waiting while going through your storm(s)? Do your feelings confuse and overwhelm you, and are they too much to process? I found solace while incorporating Kingdom principles I have encountered: strength, peace, joy, and life to continue in my faith walk. Although sometimes wavering, the courage to forgive, along with my favorite Scripture Philippians 4:13 (NKJV), which says, "I CAN do all things through Christ who strengthens me," helps me to make it through daily.

I continue to use the power of prayer, vision, mustard seed faith, internal work, and fasting while walking in the clarity that only comes from the Lord. Live your life with integrity, honesty, humility, love, hope, peace ... and FUN, knowing that God is always by your side! Life is too short to wake up with any regrets. God wants us to enjoy and live it to the fullest in Him. Treat others how you would want to be treated by showing love even to your enemies. Forgive the ones who don't or didn't show love in return. Let God handle it on your behalf. I promise that you will have a blessed outcome.

Believe that everything happens for a reason and according to God's will. When you get a second chance, grab it with both hands. If it changes your life for the good, let it. Nobody said life would be easy, but God promised it would be worth it!

God's Balm for My Bomb!
Rev. Mary L. Wilson

It was a beautiful Winter Day in February 1992 in Washingon, DC. The tiny purple crocuses were blossoming in yards in my neighborhood. I even did a little twirl in my neighbor's front yard as my five-month-pregnant belly absorbed the sun's radiance. My four children and my husband were ecstatic with the anticipation of a new addition to our family. My husband had a vision that our beautiful baby was a chocolate-hued girl, and her name would be Eboné. We spoke of her and included her name and presence in our conversations. Her siblings and cousins bought toys and gifts. We were absolutely giddy at the thought of her joining our large family.

I was almost 40 years old and was confronted by quizzical and not-so-well-meaning people who questioned my age and the number of children I already had. Some even asked, "You're pregnant AGAIN?" I ignored every naysayer and evil comment and celebrated the GOOD NEWS of NEW LIFE!

Two days after my front yard happy dance, our world was shattered by the deafening silence and lack of movement in my womb. I reasoned that she was extra sleepy and lethargic, but NOTHING I did made her move! I got on my knees and tried to position myself upside down, but still, no movement ... I prayed that I was imagining the situation ... but STILL, no movement. I was numb and in despair at the thought of the worst!

An emergency visit to the doctor for an ultrasound confirmed our deepest fear ... Eboné had no heartbeat! A bomb had exploded in my life! Our world felt shattered and blown to bits! To add to my devastation, we had to wait three days for a date at the hospital to have her delivered. I was numb with disbelief, but for some reason, I could still eat and sleep with a sense of peace. My family did all they could to support me and make me comfortable. When the word got out, prayers of intercession circulated in prayer circles and within our congregation ... but I was too numb to pray. I had to depend on the prayers of others. It was a task for me to breathe and exist, so I HAD to rely on the prayers of others. I was strangely without emotions. I just wanted to survive my traumatic and tragic ordeal.

I wanted to be angry with God for allowing such a tragedy to happen to me, one who always tried to honor and please God. I was, after all, the one who ministered to others and gave hope to hundreds of people in my life! I was the epitome of faith and hope! I preached and taught others to have hope, have faith, be optimistic; God WILL make a way; look up and live! And here I was ... NUMB!

I checked into the hospital on Monday morning, which was three days later. The procedure to induce labor took longer than I expected. By Tuesday morning, she was delivered into a world she would never know. I was so nervous about what to expect. What would she look like? Could I contain my emotions? The hospital staff was amazing and comforting. They wrapped her in a blanket and let us hold her as long as we wanted to. She had a cute little chocolate face and looked JUST like me!

When I was taken to my room, I asked for no calls or visitors. I had to come to terms on my own to try to balance myself. It was hard to concentrate or even THINK about my tomorrow. The nuns came by and read a prayer for me, and I found a sense of comfort in that. When they left, I randomly opened the Bible and tried something I'd heard the 'saints' talk about. I opened it and blindly pointed to Isaiah 61:1–3 (NKJV).

"The Spirit of the Lord God *is* upon Me,
Because the Lord has anointed Me
To preach good tidings to the poor;
He has sent Me to [a]heal the brokenhearted,
To proclaim liberty to the captives,
And the opening of the prison to *those who are* bound;
2 To proclaim the acceptable year of the Lord,
And the day of vengeance of our God;
To comfort all who mourn,
3 To [b]console those who mourn in Zion,
To give them beauty for ashes,
The oil of joy for mourning,
The garment of praise for the spirit of heaviness;
That they may be called trees of righteousness,
The planting of the Lord, that He may be glorified."

AT THAT MOMENT, a revelation from GOD detonated into my distress and grief! God delivered a BALM to me right there in my hospital room. Tears of gratitude and grace began to flow, and I was assured there was a purpose for my pain and suffering. It was a true breakthrough and a deep consolation that gave me a new promise for my life.

Until my 'bomb' went off, I was a dutiful 'First Lady' of the Union Temple Baptist Church in Washington, D.C. I taught Sunday School; created curricula for various classes; founded and directed a world-renowned Youth Choir; traveled the world, singing and ministering; and was a featured speaker for professional organizations. Often, when I would speak, individuals would approach me and say, "I KNOW you are a preacher; I hear it in your voice!" I would chuckle and tell them, "That is NOT MY CALLING!" I have always been unconventional and never wanted to fall into ANY pattern—especially in the church! Let me sit in my seat in the congregation and wear what the choir is wearing. I soundly rejected any notion of me being a 'co-pastor' to my pastor/husband!

A bomb? Me? I have always understood that a bomb is a destructive and devastating device. When I was a child growing up in Buffalo, New York, we experienced frightening, periodic air raid bomb drills. We would lay our heads on our desks and put our arms over our heads. We did not know the seriousness of our potential situation, but we did as we were told.

So, what IS a bomb? It is a devastating explosive device designed to cause massive destruction and arrest the development of systems. Anyone in the range of a bomb can be affected. Bombs can be planned by enemies or naturally occurring events. They can also clear out a large area for future development. Watching a building implode can be a satisfying sight because it usually is followed by a new, often exciting construction of a new building.

How can there be a balm that will mitigate or heal the devastation of a bomb? A balm is an ointment intended to heal and relieve suffering and infections. In most cases, a balm is not usually recommended for severe, life-altering situations and illnesses. At this point, I began to formulate the idea that my bomb had a clear directive—to clear a path for my destiny and purpose in life. I wanted to be angry and rebellious toward God. Still, the clear message in Isaiah confirmed God's will for my life.

After a graveside service for Eboné, I committed to six weeks of physical, emotional, and spiritual recovery. I meditated, prayed, and read life-affirming materials for the entire time. My loving husband and family surrounded me while I navigated this new normal. I had to answer many questions and ignore many thoughtless comments—including those who said, "Well, at least you still have other children!"

A few months after my bomb hit, I started to understand what was REALLY happening in my life. I realized God had been preparing me to operate FULLY in my power! Yes, I was a mother! Yes, I was a wife! Yes, I was an effective and capable first lady! Yes, I had created a choir of over 100 nationally known youth! But I had NOT answered my ultimate call to be in ministry. God spoke to me, loud and clear, and said that He wanted me IN POSITION! I was to birth and deliver my MINISTRY—IN THE PULPIT—NEXT TO MY HUSBAND! The baby I needed was not flesh and blood but obedience to God's purpose and will for my life!

I want to encourage anyone who has suffered the loss of a baby through miscarriage, abortion, or infertility with these words: GOD HAS A BALM FOR YOUR BOMB. God has not forgotten or forsaken you. He will cause your pain to pay you! The Lord will cause the earth to yield its harvest, and God, your God, will bless you. His purpose and plans for you still stand. Never forget that the Lord is always with you, upholding you with His victorious right hand.

Faith in the Father: Released from Orphan to Daughterhood
Dr. KeyShaze Ward

Abused. Abandoned. Rejected. Neglected. Unprotected. Feeling alone. Unsure of life and uncertain of who you are. All of those things led me to think like an orphan. I had a family but felt like an orphan. That is the story of the early years of my life.

So, let's start from the beginning. I felt like Sophia in *The Color Purple* when she said, "All my life, I had to fight." My mom, a domestic violence survivor, says that I was prematurely born because she had pre-eclampsia, and physical violence caused her to go into labor. So, you can imagine that the devil wanted to take me out at birth. I grew up in church, so I knew of God and that I needed to receive Jesus so I wouldn't go to hell. (My grandfather was an apostolic pastor who preached heaven or hell.) I lived in the projects and thought life was good. My single mother raising three children on welfare was doing her best. She walked us to church, stood at the bus stop with me when I went to kindergarten, and ensured we were fed and cared for. But life for us seemed to change when she met a fellow.

Once we moved into a bigger apartment in the projects, and this person was now a part of our lives, life was no longer the same. This person seemed to now have control, including disciplining my siblings and me. It wasn't until my mom took my grandmother on a trip and we stayed home with this person that his true colors showed; he molested me. And I always say that had my mom not called to check in, there is no telling how far this person would have gone with a 10-year-old. Then he uttered those famous words, "Don't tell your mama." From that moment, I ran up to the room with my sister and stayed there.

I would try to stay as far away from this person as possible, but he lived with us. I will never forget going to school that Monday and feeling as if my classmates knew something because a fellow 5th grader, with her nasty mouth, said, "Someone's daddy is playing with their pXXXy." As I reflect on that moment, I wonder, "Was I giving off some sort of red flag?" and even more significant, "Was that happening to her or even someone else in the class?" I am now thinking back and wondering if that began my journey of not liking or wanting to be around people. For a long time, when I didn't want to be bothered with people, I found ways not to be around them.

Thinking back, it wasn't as much about the molestation as it was about the demon the devil had set up in our lives. I absolutely hated this person. I even said it one time, and my mom whooped me. Her response was, "He gives you quarters for school," not realizing at the time that this person violated and crossed a line with her young daughter that should never be crossed, especially since he was a 'father figure,' using that term loosely. It was not until we visited one of his sons in jail that his daughter (much older than us from a previous relationship), riding with us, said, "If anyone is touching you, tell your mother." WOW! As I write this, it is sparking so many spiritual revelations that God knows how to communicate with us, even in our young age! In essence, He was saying to speak up and say something!

At that point, I told my sister, and we went to tell my mom that same day. My mom was furious, and I believe she left the house for a moment. While she was out, he came to me and said, "I hope you didn't lie on me." It seemed from that moment I felt that this person tried everything to 'take our mom away from us.' His actions caused me to become increasingly angry and resentful, and might I venture to say hateful, as life got hard for my siblings and me.

He moved us from the projects; I remember living from house to house because bills were not being paid. He would open businesses (e.g., clubs and restaurants). I would have to care for my siblings until the wee hours of the morning. We often didn't have food or had to wait for my mom to bring us food from 'the restaurant.' We didn't always have running water, so we had to use gallon jugs of water to wash up in these gray restaurant pans and use that same water to get the toilet to flush. So many things happened to me, to us, that space and time do not permit elaboration, like meeting my dad at 10 years old. Remember that son we visited in jail earlier? Well, he came to live with us, and I lost my virginity at 13 years old; he was 26. Since the devil couldn't use the father, he used the son. That is another story for another time.

The cycle of terror followed me into my teenage years. And it seemed the older I got, this person became more and more hateful toward me. I became a fighter, handling things with my fists, not because I wanted to, but because it somehow became my reputation (SMH!). Anyway, he came home from the club (he owned) drunk and acted like I had left the light on in my room. I was always awake because I never knew what to expect when he and my mom got home from the club. I said, "I just watched you turn that light on." He was furious! So, I got up and started going toward my chest of drawers. My mom knew I was not going there for clothes; I kept weapons. She told me to get dressed and that we were going to my grandmother's house. He grabbed me. I was fighting, as my mom was pulling me out of the house, and he was trying to pull me back into the house. To this day, I have the scrape on my foot as a reminder of that night. We got to my grandmother's and stayed there for a few days. After we returned home, I discovered I was pregnant at 15 years old. My son is one of THE BEST things that happened to me because his presence calmed me in a way that set me on a path of seeing life differently.

However, because this person always said that I wouldn't be anything, being a teen parent, he felt, made him right about me. I graduated a year early from high school, and 'adult' life at 16 started, as I was out of the house and on my own. Thank God for my boyfriend's (now my husband's) parents because they cared for our son for the first two years of his life, as I was living from pillar to post, with nowhere to go. That is how I ended up in the U.S. Navy at 17. God allowed people and experiences in my life to lead me down that path. I didn't join because I wanted to serve my country (LOL!). I joined because I needed a consistent place to stay. Although I was out of the house, I still visited my mom and had to see and deal with this person. As I got older, he hated seeing me come around because he felt I could influence my mom to walk away from him. A mess!

I said all this to say, what happens when the people God entrusted to protect you on the earth, through their actions, cause you to feel abandoned, rejected, etc.? While molestation is a horrible experience for the victims, it is even more traumatic when you feel like no one believes you or those you expect to protect and be your voice (your advocate) seem to go silent. Or, you get the 'feeling' that it should never be talked about again because it's over. You become one who gets really good at keeping secrets, even when they are to your detriment, especially when you are already 'the quiet one.' What happens when your voice is silenced as a child?

My experiences have taught me that when children undergo trauma, it is the enemy's way of silencing them before they reach their full potential. The devil thinks that if he can stop or stunt your growth as a youth, the likelihood of you getting to where God wants you to be will be slim to none. BUT THE DEVIL IS A LIAR! The blessing is that God knows us from our mother's womb, and He sanctifies and calls us! So, no matter what the enemy tries at birth and even in our childhood, God is with us! We shall be ALL that God has called us to be! So, YOU, yeah, YOU! Come out, be loosed, and be free in Jesus' name!

As a child, you don't know about the spiritual battle for your life; as a result, anger, bitterness, resentment, and hatred begin to settle in. You find yourself isolating. You find yourself in survival mode, trying to make it from day to day because it appears that no one cares; it's every man (or woman) for themselves. But through these words, my prayer is that someone will find the courage they need to break out of the bondage of isolation and be free. I DID; so can you! To God Be The Glory. May the healing balm of Jesus Christ heal and deliver you from the scars of the past; heal you from the pain of what didn't happen, what did happen; and help you to forgive them for what they did or didn't do. Unforgiveness is killing you! It was killing me!

Quite frankly, I had to go through the process of forgiving my mother. We all hold our mothers in such high esteem, and no one wants to be mad at their mother. My mom is the nicest, most beautiful person I know. But I realized that I resented her. I was angry with my mother for subjecting us to this person, even after she knew what he had done to me. As I walked through my journey, I understood that our parents do the best they can with the knowledge they have. Truthfully, many of us quickly say what we would or wouldn't do in a situation until life presents us with the same challenges, and we must walk in another person's shoes. However, when I tell you that God can redeem the times and create beautiful relationships, my mother and father are my biggest cheerleaders and supporters. I know they love me very much! And guess what? I love them back!

With that said, some may wonder, how did you get to the place of forgiveness when you felt such anger, bitterness, hatred, and resentment? Let me be the first to tell you that FORGIVING IS HARD, especially when you have been violated, abused, and mistreated. But there were some things that God allowed me to learn. My first lesson was actually from Joyce Myer. Years ago, she shared her testimony about forgiving her father, who violated her. She said it was a daily decision. I had to make a conscious, daily decision to forgive.

Another thing that I learned was what the Word of God says about forgiveness. Matthew 18 is rich with instructions on how to forgive. However, what stuck with me was: 1) God will not forgive us if we don't forgive. How many of us are in danger of not being forgiven by God because we choose not to forgive? I also learned that I have not always been nice to others, and I'm sure people also had to forgive me. 2) When we don't forgive, we are turned over to the tormentors, like the servant who received forgiveness but would not forgive. As a result of my unforgiveness, I dealt with stomach issues because I was always mad at somebody or about something, in addition to being angry at my violator and my mother. It was so bad; I took stomach medication for at least three years.

It takes energy to be angry, bitter, and resentful! It is stressful to live that way all the time. It is a miserable place to be. So, as I hope you can begin to see, it was far beyond the situation and the people; it became about me and my need for Jesus to come and heal me! Oh, but God! When I chose to forgive and let the anger, bitterness, and hatred go, I can tell you that I have not had to take stomach medication for that issue in years. How many of us are dealing with health issues or other issues (relationship failures, isolation, etc.) because we choose to wallow in the mud of anger, hatred, resentment, and bitterness? Folks, I realized I was not living the life God had ordained for me. Oh, but the testimony gets better.

Jeremiah 29:11 is true when it says, "For I know the thoughts that I think toward you, saith the LORD, thoughts of peace, and not of evil, to give you an expected end." (NKJV) The glory is not that my perpetrator had to watch me excel as an overcomer; every negative word became fuel to make the devil out of a liar. The glory is in the power of God, who allowed these experiences to shape me into the woman I am today. I'm not going to say that life has always been kind, but I can say that every experience began me on a journey of finding Jesus and learning who HE is for me. I had to seek God! I needed God!

These negative experiences damaged how I saw myself and skewed my view of who I was. I felt like an orphan. God had to 'Fix My Faulty Filters™.' I didn't see myself as God saw me. But I tell you what, God began to speak to me in prayer. He helped me see Him as ABBA, God my Father!

As I read His Word, it would minister to me how important I am to Him and, most importantly, that HE LOVES ME, flaws and all! One of my favorite Scriptures is I John 3:2, which says, "Beloved, now are we the sons of God, and it doth not yet appear what we shall be: but we know that, when He shall appear, we shall be like Him; for we shall see Him as He is." (KJV) As Jesus began to heal me, my prayers became different, so much so that I prayed for the one who violated me. I realized that every soul is important to God, regardless of what they have done. That is the epitome of John 3:16! I understood that this journey on earth is temporary, but eternity is forever.

Furthermore, you know that you are walking in forgiveness when you realize that a person's soul is more important than what they did to hurt you. In 2 Peter 3:9 (paraphrased), the Word tells us that God wishes that none should perish, but all should come to repentance. So, I prayed that this person would receive Jesus in his heart. As God matured me to this level of prayer, I also learned that God will vindicate us. A few months before this person died, my mom called me and said that the person had told her what he had done to me. I told her that if he had the courage to confess to her, then that meant that God was working on his heart. I told her that I had already forgiven the person, not realizing he would die months later. I prayed that he made peace with God and that eternal life with the Lord is his portion.

As I reflect on that part of my life and write this chapter, I realize that even in my youth, my stupidity, and folly, God has always been there to get me to where I am now and to take me to where I am going. He has been by my side! Psalm 139:8 is true when it says, "If we make our bed in hell, thou (God) art there." He is with us through the oppression and the struggle, and He assigns His angelic host to watch us. So, when I look back over my life, God has been the constant, and I forever owe God my life. Because He saved my life! God saved my life!

I could be anything … I should be homeless and still living from pillar to post. I should have and could have been almost anything. But "the master of the sea heard my despairing cry, from the water He lifted me, now safe am I!"[5] Please know that when God has a purpose for our lives, NOTHING and NO ONE can stop what God has designed, for He sees us as we SHALL BE, like HIM! And even when I was running rampant, and my upbringing wasn't all that great, God saw me in His image in the midst of all of it! MY GOD! To Him be glory, forever and ever!

I close by praying for someone who may have found themselves lost in the cruelty of life. Perhaps you have been trying to escape the hole of abandonment, resentment, anger, violation, betrayal, and the like. As you read this prayer, I want you to surrender all the pain and the hurt to God. HE CAN HANDLE IT! If you have to cry, go ahead and scream if you must, but go after your freedom.

---

[5]https://hymnary.org/text/i_was_sinking_deep_in_sin_far_from_the

In the name of Jesus Christ, I pray that at this moment, Lord, bring someone into total freedom and deliverance. Father, deal with the demonic force that torments them with the pain of abuse, violation, and hurt. Your Word tells us in James 4:7 that as we submit ourselves to You, we can RESIST the devil, and he must flee from us. So, I pray that my sister/brother will submit to You. May they gain the strength to tell the devil to leave their life now and never return. I pray that You will give them the strength and the courage to let go so they can experience a different life filled with peace and joy. Fill them now with Your Spirit in the name of Jesus. As my sister (brother) cries out to You, give them the strength and courage to forgive and release their violator and forgive the one(s) who abandoned them. Thank You, Lord, for sending the healing balm of Jesus Christ and for setting my sister (brother) on a path to wholeness. You are no respecter of persons, and You who helped me are FULLY CAPABLE to help them. Thank You, dear Father, for allowing them to see You in a new way and for setting them free to be all You have designed and created them to be. No more letting their situation, hurt, and pain hold them back. It's time to move forward! Thank You, Father, in Jesus' name! AMEN!

Save Your Daughter
Chaplain Paulette McPherson

A mother's love endures through all.
—Washington Irving

Like many women of color, I had a complicated relationship with my mother. While I knew she loved me, how she expressed her love sometimes left me feeling unloved and rejected. On one of the days when I had no doubt let her down, she proclaimed that I was not planned and that her friends had told her not to have me at nearly 39 years old. Wait, what? Who were these friends, as Mom didn't even have that many friends, and why would they tell her to abort me? More to the point, why in the world would she tell me? Her words pierced me like a burning bullet, much like other statements eluding to the fact that I would never amount to anything, or that I wasn't educated like her friends' daughters who could seemingly do no wrong, or that me giving my life to Christ as a young teenager would not last.

My mom was uber smart, and anything she put her hand to was a masterpiece; she did it all to a high standard: crochet, sewing, knitting, cooking. I loved her creativity, sense of humor and sarcasm, classy style, and how others loved her. But there were times I secretly hated how she made me feel. I hated that she spoke well of my siblings, but I never heard her speak well of me. I hated that I could not talk to her about 'things.' Most importantly, I hated the day when she found me in my 'slip' at the age of six after a family member had touched me inappropriately; I hated that she made me feel dirty; I hated that we never spoke about it; I hated that she made me feel like it was my fault; and I hated that I was told to 'get dressed' as though nothing happened.

From a young age, I internalized feelings of shame and worthlessness, which led to low self-esteem, feelings that my views were unimportant, and the inability to label and verbalize my emotions and speak up appropriately. I developed a lack of trust in others and my own judgment. Being raised in a strict West Indian home came with its own rules, and Mom, the disciplinarian in our house, had very high standards. My parents didn't have the best marriage, and Mom started planning to move back to Jamaica. As the time grew closer for Mom to leave, she shared with me her plans for the school that I would attend, one where I spent the week in school and only came home at the weekends. I remember thinking I would rather dig my eyes out with a rusty spoon than be in a strange country, living with strangers and mosquitos, only coming home once weekly; no, thanks! I knew there was a God somewhere, and maybe Mom did love me after all because she delayed her exit from England. She eventually moved back to the West Indies when I was 16, leaving me in England with my family.

Although I knew she was leaving, it tore me apart. It widened the gap in our mother-daughter relationship, sprinkling rejection and abandonment seeds on my already vulnerable life. I nurtured the fully grown plants of rejection and abandonment for 38 years. It wasn't until I started training to become a Chaplain did it dawn on me that Mom may not have said she loved me, still her actions spoke louder than her words, as I finally realized she stayed in a marriage for more years than she had planned, only leaving when she felt I was old enough to be somewhat independent. That's love.

After Mom left England, I lived with my sister-in-law's mother, Sister Hutton. It was funny that her first name was Dorinda, and my mom was Dorenda. Ms. Dorinda was quite the opposite of Mom; she was more laid back. I could talk to her about absolutely anything, and she would offer guidance in her gentle, amusing way. We often sat up until the early hours, eating junk and talking about Scripture, church, movies, and hair. She took the sting out of the last four years of being a teenager. She was so approachable that I remember speaking to her about a young man I liked in church, a good friend, who everyone thought I was dating ... church folk! John came from a family that reminded me of "The Waltons." He was the second youngest of seven boys of Elder and Sister McPherson. I knew his brothers before I knew of him, as they were known for telling people they were related to the gospel group 'The Winans.' When John joined the church, he perpetuated the untruth too, if anyone would ask, sometimes with a fake American accent. One day in church, a particularly annoying young lady asked me in the presence of John and some of his brothers if they were related to the Winans family. With a straight face, I said it was true to get rid of her ... God forgive me! That was an open door for John and me to talk, as we laughed about it for months. I was attracted to John because he was focused, funny, a born leader, and a really cool dude. We started dating in 1988, and in September of 1989, we got married when I was 20 and he was 21.

I adore everything about Christmas, and on December 7, 1993, I knew that this particular Christmas would be one I would never forget. John and I waited some years before starting our family. I was seven months pregnant with our first child, and I would typically bathe before bedtime to relax in the hope that I would sleep through the night. Typically, the baby would kick when the warm water hit its body, but I felt no kick that night. I tapped my belly several times and filled the bath with more hot water—to the point that only a person with skin made of asbestos could tolerate the temperature—in an attempt to wake the baby; surely, baby was sleeping. As I lay in the bath, worrying and praying simultaneously, I remembered a documentary I had watched about women who had experienced stillbirths the previous month. Surely, this could not possibly be my plight. Fortunately, I had an appointment at the clinic the following morning so they could confirm why I couldn't feel the baby moving around. It was the longest 15 minutes of my life, and the silence was deafening. The sonographer scanned and scanned my stomach in complete silence and then called the doctor in to also conduct a scan. The doctor confirmed my worst nightmare; my baby had died. I remember the doctor and me going back and forth about how the baby would be delivered. I insisted on a C-section, and he insisted that the baby's life was no longer at risk; therefore, a C-section was off the table, as it was a life-saving procedure.

My mind was blank; I feared death and was walking around with a dead baby. That afternoon, my labor was induced, and after the longest 36 hours of my life, Nathan James McPherson was delivered in silence on the evening of December 9, 1993, weighing in at two pounds. We left the hospital silently the next day without balloons, flowers, or a baby. One week later, we laid Nathan James to rest in the frigid cold in a grave the week before Christmas. The weather was so cold that I remember wanting to return to the cemetery and retrieve my baby because 'he was cold.'

Two years later, I was pregnant again. The pregnancy was complicated, resulting in me having pre-eclampsia. Here I was, seven months pregnant again, and a routine scan and blood tests revealed some chromosome disorder in our unborn child, and I was given three options. The first option was to have an amniocentesis, a test performed by inserting a needle through the mother's abdomen to withdraw some of the amniotic fluid to assess the fetus's chromosomes. Option two was to have a late-term abortion, and option three was to wait and see what happens at the birth. As the tears rolled down my face, the doctors spoke about the possibility of the baby having Down syndrome, cystic fibrosis, or another chromosome disorder.

On receiving the news, I went home, and lying on the floor in front of the fireplace, I cried and prayed to God to perform a miracle. My godmother, Sister Redhead, had instilled in me at an early age the power of prayer, and I always believed in miracles. How could I be in the same situation of losing another child so late in the pregnancy? A wise pastor's wife once told me, "You can't worry and pray simultaneously; you have to do one or the other." So, day and night, I would lie on the floor and call out to God on my baby's behalf, as I didn't have the emotional fortitude to bury a second child.

We had to go back to the hospital for yet another scan. In the meantime, we received a letter from the hospital reiterating what they told us at the initial diagnosis. The day finally arrived, and they scanned me extensively, only to conclude that what they initially saw on the scan and subsequently confirmed in writing was no longer there. As the old folks used to say in testimony service, "Whom could it be?" The doctors were in utter shock and could not explain it; they were speechless, confused, and embarrassed; I, on the other hand, gave God thanks for being the great physician and miracle worker. My only daughter, Chantelle, was born with no sickness or complications at 36-week gestation, weighing in at 5lbs 9oz.

I know that children don't come with batteries or instructions; you have to figure out the parenting plan on the fly. Chantelle was always a daddy's girl before #GirlDad started to trend after the death of Kobe Bryant and his daughter Gianna in 2020. As Chantelle grew, I was aware of the importance of her having a father figure in her life. But it was equally important for me to be her nurturer, as I felt I had not been nurtured. Unlike my experiences growing up, I tried to model healthy ways when resolving conflict in the home; still, the boundaries can become indistinct, and it was clear that she started to choose one parent over the other early on. Over the years, Chantelle was made to believe she and her younger brother (Jonathan—six years apart) were the most important people in her father's life, and I took second place. Unfortunately, as parents, we didn't present a united front, and her power shift came when she could control the narrative with her father and disregard me as her mother.

Over the years, the pain from our intense interactions was indescribable; I wanted desperately to be close to my only daughter, and the only time that happened was if she was sick. History had repeated itself; not only was there a glaring gap in our mother-daughter relationship, but here I was again, unable to use my voice to express my feelings. The body keeps a score, and my internalized emotional pain and anguish manifested physically through migraines, digestion issues, and lethargy. At my wit's end, I scheduled a conference with my bishop to discuss my toxic home life, and amongst other things, he told me, "Save your daughter." Save my daughter from what or who? What the heck? Did he not hear anything I told him about her constant disrespect and passive-aggressive undermining behavior? I was at a loss for words, but every time I disagreed with my daughter, I heard his voice reminding me to save my daughter.

Over the years, our heated interactions would ebb and flow, and I increasingly distrusted her, her brother, and her father. During one heated argument, I snapped and felt like my no-nonsense West-Indian mother for the first time. The years of anger and frustration of suppressing my emotions and not using my voice in my childhood and my adult relationships blew the lid clear off my emotional tank, and before I knew it, I had laid hands on her, and not the church type with oil; before I blinked, I heard a symphony of sirens, and there were multiple police cars outside our home in our predominantly white neighborhood. The proverbial had hit the fan, and I was sitting on the sofa, surrounded by police and rocking like rain man, repeating, "I'm tired; I told her to shut up. I'm the mother, and I can't take anymore." I was a hot mess, and I could not believe I had allowed myself to get to this point. I silently waited for the police to put me in handcuffs in the back of a police car, with my bad hair day—can you imagine the mugshot? But they didn't; instead, they suggested that my daughter and I attend a crisis center program to rebuild our relationship.

Chantelle left home for a while, and although I wasn't in a physical prison, it felt like I was in an emotional one for months, as I did not know whether I would be charged with assault. The enemy of my soul replayed every possible news headline in my mind. I began to shut down slowly, still unable to verbalize the trauma. I had hit rock bottom. Where did I go wrong, and how could my flesh and blood despise me after all I had sacrificed to bring her into the world and raise her in a godly environment? I know you can't fight spirit with flesh; this was spiritual warfare.

In any battle, you have to know yourself and your weaknesses, and you have to know your enemy. My weakness was that my self-esteem, self-confidence, and sanity had been weakened and worn down over the years, and I lost my ability to fight back. I had allowed the enemy of my soul to mess around with my thought process, shatter my confidence, and keep his finger on my mute button. He used family members to use a slow drip-to-destruction tactic, gaslighting, as a weapon against me. According to Merriam-Webster, *gaslighting is the psychological manipulation of a person, usually over an extended period, that causes the victim to question the validity of their thoughts, perception of reality, or memories and typically leads to confusion, loss of confidence and self-esteem, the uncertainty of one's emotional or mental stability.*

After years of being physically, mentally, and emotionally tired, I eventually stopped fighting with my daughter. I started praying "Lord, you see; Lord, you hear; and Lord, you will answer" as my daily mantra when issues arose. I cannot lie; it has been an uphill struggle and taken years to finally reach a healthy point in my relationship with my daughter where I trust her. I am so thankful to God for a 180-degree turnaround, and I credit it to the Holy Spirit.

As I mentioned earlier, Christmas is my favorite time of the year. I received this letter from my daughter for Christmas of 2022:

Dear Mommy, where do I begin? First, I want to say thank you & I love you. That's honestly all I've been saying this past year daily. I wouldn't be here if it weren't for you. This past year has opened my eyes to why you're my mommy & how much I need you. How much I needed you in the past, now, present & future ... I'm always going to need you. For times when I want to give up, I'm going to need you. For my future bridal shopping, I'm going to need you. I want you at all the events, Mommy, all of them. As a little girl, I would get jealous seeing friends & family hanging out with their moms & going on trips or doing fun things, especially during my teen years & even now. I always wanted that but was scared to ask; I assumed it wouldn't happen ... (sigh). I want to apologize for how I was growing up; you didn't deserve it at all. I acted a certain way & at times; I would cry because I just wanted a great relationship with my mommy. After last year & noticing the crazy things we've been through, I'm so glad to call you my mommy & to be called your daughter. You never stopped fighting for me & all I can say is thank you. I still, at times, think I don't deserve it, seriously. Sometimes I feel like the worst daughter but thank you for your patience. I thank you for your prayers. I thank you for your love. I thank you for your discerning spirit. I thank you for the lessons you taught me. I thank you for everything. I truly do. The pain you've been through because of me; my goodness. I'm sorry. I've caused so much hurt, & I know you say it's okay, & you're just happy we communicate now, but it hurts me sometimes. To realize I said awful things to you & about you. Ugh! I want to cry... I get mad. You deserve the world & then some. God knew what He was doing when He created you. He took His time because you're one of a kind. You're so special. I'm repeating myself, but I don't know how to repay you for all the hurt & pain I put you through. I'm doing my best to build our relationship & make it stronger than ever. I want nothing but the absolute BEST for you. Every single day, I work hard for you, Mommy. You keep my head held high. You make me realize how strong of a woman I can & will be. I want to show you that I love you & that we deserve one another. I want to give you the world.

> *I love you, Mommy. Always have & always will. I love you, Queen.*
> *Love, Your Princess*

Admittedly, when I received the letter, my heart raced at the mini epistle typed in single space 10 font *and* laminated. I instantly thought, *More drama; what have I done now?* I skimmed it and responded accordingly, as my daughter was present. It took me a few weeks to read it thoroughly and process its contents. Since the letter, I have had moments when I thought she might revert to being who she was before. I was prepared to have a distant relationship with her for self-preservation; however, she has been constant in her relationship with me. Chantelle is a strong, resilient, intelligent, loving, funny, and beautiful young lady, and I am beyond proud of her. We speak most days, and she shares her thoughts and experiences with me, as mothers and daughters should.

Admittedly, I am a 'church snob,' as I don't particularly like high fiving my neighbor or talking to them during service. I blame it on my British upbringing and COVID. However, if I had to say something to a neighbor, it would be "I can see clearly now the rain has gone" (Johnny Nash). I had cataract surgery on both my natural eyes not long ago because of my impaired vision; the difference in my eyesight is now night and day. Trusting God to remove spiritual cataracts is also miraculous, doesn't cost $5,000, and is life changing.

The enemy's tactics blinded me. Hindsight is a beautiful thing, and I would encourage anyone who is in the type of toxic relationship that I was in with not just my daughter but also my son and husband to seek a good family therapist that will provide psychotherapy (talk therapy) focusing on improving interfamilial behaviors and relationships.

Your family unit may look different from mine, consisting of parents/guardians, siblings, grandparents, aunts and uncles, caregivers, etc., but pray about finding the right one to help you with issues like relationship conflicts, new life changes (e.g., medical or moving house), and dead parent-child/sibling conflict. As you combine therapy with prayer and fasting, I want to encourage you further to save your daughter, son, brother, sister, parent(s), or friend;

don't give up. When you get tired, learn to rest, but never give up. Remember, some miracles are instantaneous, and some are a work in progress.

Today, through therapy (lots of it), lifestyle changes, and prayer, I am daily uprooting anything that has wrapped itself around my future, destiny, and God-given purpose. I declare that I am on the road to being healthy, whole, and healed and that no one in my bloodline will experience such trauma again. I am blessed that my job as a Chaplain allows me to help others find their voice and purpose by pulling to the side of life's road to realign themselves after hitting a pothole of doubt and fear. I could not have made it this far by myself, and I am so thankful for my friends who supported me throughout my darkest hours when I hit rock bottom. From now on, the only way is upward and onward.

Nurturing Faith from Sorrow to Serenity
Deborah Johnson

My story began in 2019 when I decided that I needed to make some changes. I tried to hang in there for as long as I could. A part of me was holding on to what people would think while considering my children's feelings and how they would adjust. After all, this was one of the most difficult decisions I had to make in my entire life. I am one of the bishop's daughters, the oldest of three, and the first of my siblings to get married, yet my marriage was falling apart.

I thought my life was pretty good. I had a good job and was doing well for myself. I got married in 2006, had our daughter three years later in 2009, and our son came six years later in 2015. Yet, after 13 years of marriage, I could not pretend to be OK anymore. I started looking for places to live so that my two children and I wouldn't be living out of my car. I had mentally checked out long before I made the decision to end my marriage.

THE ILLUSION

Every little girl dreams of living a fairytale life, thanks to the entertainment industry. Movies and television programs do a great job of conditioning viewers to desire a life that quite frankly is not real. Life is not a movie, neither is it your favorite family television show. As a new mom, I was under the impression that I would be spoiled, getting things that I wanted and being catered to. That's every pregnant girl's dream, right? Well, that didn't happen for me. To be completely honest, most of the time, I would do things on my own because I was so independent. I wanted things when I wanted them. I can admit I was spoiled (thanks, Dad). It became more difficult, especially the closer I got to my due date. Being as independent as I was, I did not allow my husband at the time to take the lead as I should have. Looking back, I could have done better. I was in my own way. If I wanted something done, I wanted it done right away. I did not want to wait until it was convenient for him. Don't get me wrong; there were times he responded immediately. But remember, I am a daddy's girl, and I am spoiled.

Let's go a little deeper. I was independent and immature. I am sharing that because I have had to learn to be patient and to ask for help. I can recall being pregnant during the winter and not wanting to wait until my husband at the time came home to clear the sidewalk of snow. So I took my pregnant self outside and started shoveling snow because I wanted a visible walkway right then. Impatience can be dangerous. My neighbors noticed what I was doing and came out. They were adamant about me going into the house to relax. They told me they would take care of it and asked why I was outside. My response to them was that it needed to be done before the temperature dropped, or it would have been worse. I am grateful that God protected me and my daughter. I was truly blessed to have some amazing neighbors that didn't mind helping, even when I didn't ask.

On May 27, 2009, my life changed dramatically when my daughter was born. She was my world. She was my everything. My focus had shifted from me, and my full attention turned to our daughter. I will forever cherish my family's help. My sister came and stayed with me for about three months to help with the adjustment of a newborn. She was God-sent. Her support helped me get through all the tiredness and adjustments when it was time to return to work. It also allowed my sister to bond with her niece. I am so thankful for my sister coming to assist me. When it was time for her to return home, I was an emotional wreck. I didn't want her to leave us. She did a great job spoiling me and her niece.

My focus remained on our daughter as she got older. I never fully shifted back into wife mode because I felt like I was her only protector. In retrospect, that was another lesson I learned. I was so into being a mother that being a spouse took a back seat. I am grateful to God for the awareness. Back then, I just didn't understand that.

My daughter was with me all the time. If you saw me, you saw her. I was determined to be a super mom. That illusion was quickly shattered when my daughter was two years old. My husband at the time and I were in the Poconos, celebrating our 5th Wedding Anniversary. During the trip, I accidentally missed a step and broke my ankle. I was devastated. Not only did I have a traumatic injury that required major surgery with plates and screws and later a cast, I couldn't properly care for our daughter. Remember, she was two years old and getting into everything. Being the spoiled, independent, and oldest child of my parents, I called and asked them to help me with her. They were wonderful. They kept her for me during my recovery, which was about 12 weeks. What made it more difficult for me was that my parents lived two hours away, and I only saw her on the weekends for a couple of hours. Imagine my loneliness, anxiety, and despair because, remember, she had become my everything. Unfortunately, and unintentionally, I had created an awkward environment for my marriage. I own that. I was so focused on being a mother that I neglected to be as intentional about being a wife.

Once again, I was grateful that my family supported me and helped me get through that time of healing. It was the little things that made a world of difference. After my recovery, and my daughter came back home, I went right back to being independent, controlling and wanting things my way. Facing this truth now, I can laugh about it. It wasn't funny then. I alienated my husband at the time. I really didn't know better. Truthfully, I expected him to act like my dad. Every now and then, I would let him know that I needed a break from being a super mom. Sometimes that went well; sometimes it didn't. We got through those moments, but things had certainly changed in our relationship.

We did not have the communication skills to properly address conflict, so we would just push issues under the rug. That's important to note here because our way of addressing what we needed to talk about was to not talk about it and just have sex. That's crazy, right? We were not emotionally connecting like we once did. We kept having sex, though, and my son was born in 2015. By then, I really felt like a single parent because I was doing my thing, and so was he.

As parents, we just do what's needed. We find a way to get it done. I had such unrealistic expectations. Sometimes, I would pull up in the driveway and sit in the car because I didn't want to go into the house. I became mentally and emotionally drained. Our relationship was spiraling downward, and I was miserable.

The saying that misery loves company is true. By this time in our marriage, we had put each other through a lot by omission and commission. I vividly remember the night I decided I couldn't do it anymore. I had emotionally and mentally checked out of my marriage. I was losing myself. I did not like the person I had become. My self-confidence, self-worth, and self-esteem were all nonexistent, and I was parenting my children on fumes. I was at the end of myself and knew I needed to ask for help. We tried counseling. We tried prayer. Nothing seemed to be working, so I started planning my exit strategy.

THE GRACE FOR IT

Things happen for a reason all the time. In 2019, when the children and I moved out of our home, I had to downsize to a 2-bedroom, 2-bathroom apartment where the kids had to share a room. In our old house, they each had their own. I knew the smaller living arrangement was temporary. I didn't like being in an apartment, but I had to make it work until something better came. It seemed that the fire alarm would randomly go off in the middle of the night about twice a month. I had to wake up the kids, make sure they were bundled up and warm, and stand outside in the cold until it was clear to return to the building. I hated that but had to make the best of it, knowing it was only temporary.

At least we were able to get something decent before the disruption in our family life impacted my credit negatively. That was another blessing in disguise. The move happened so quickly; I knew God was looking out for me. My faith in God grew stronger because I could only lean on Him to help me through this difficult time.

On the weekends that my kids went with their father, their return on Sunday would be emotional because they cried so much. Their hearts were broken because their parents were no longer together. Seeing them that way hurt me because I never thought I would be in this situation. I never imagined in a thousand years that I would have been married for 13 years and now separated, contemplating divorce. I prayed even harder during those times. I didn't know how they felt because I grew up in a two-parent home, so I couldn't relate. Seeing them brokenhearted each time they came home made me question if I had made the right decision. Did I do the right thing? Should I have stayed in it longer, or at least until they were grown? Each time the answer would come back that I did what was best for me and the children.

Just as things seemed to be settling down for us, I found out that my mom was diagnosed with cancer. Shortly thereafter, she began her cycle of treatments with chemotherapy and radiation at John Hopkins University Hospital. Since I was only about 15 miles away, we agreed that Mom would stay with me. Between my brother and I, we would get her to her appointments. Mom, staying with me, granted some relief, knowing I could simply focus on getting my son from daycare after I got off work. I knew my daughter was OK because Memaw, as the grandkids called her, would be waiting for her to get home from school.

My daughter often told me that she and Mom (Memaw) would go to the mall or get something to eat or some snacks before I got home. At night, our routine was going into the kids' room and doing meditations until we all fell asleep. At some point, I would get up and go in my room while Mom slept in the bed with the kids. The kids enjoyed Mom's time with us as much as I did. She went home on the weekends. I am so grateful for that quality time with my mom. God gave me the strength I needed to be strong for my mom. I continued taking her to her treatments, which was a great bonding time for us. We listened to positive music and said prayers on our way to the hospital. I would encourage her and tell her she would be OK. I would tell her often, "You got this!" While I didn't know her true emotional state during some moments in this process, I knew that she was a woman of faith and would make it because she had made it through before. This wasn't her first time being treated for cancer, and if God brought her through the first time, I had enough faith to believe He would do it again. I was hopeful. Whenever I made a post on social media, I would always end it with #ISTILLBELIEVE.

My faith was and is strong. Regardless of how things might have looked, I still believed. I trusted that God would perform a miracle in Mom's life. I believed that she was going to be healed. A few months after Mom's treatment ended, during a follow-up examination, the doctors found that the cancer had metastasized, spreading to other areas of her body, including her lungs and blood. She was getting physically weaker and had less strength. Things weren't looking so good. Nevertheless, I still believed God.

In the last weeks, before she stopped talking, I reassured her that her family would be all right and that we would make it. On December 13, 2020, my brother, sister, and I sang "Yes Jesus Loves Me" to Mom at home. She was then moved to the hospital, where she earned her wings on December 16, 2020. The day Mom transitioned felt like the world was spinning in slow motion. Even more, this was during the height of the pandemic, which meant we did not and could not have the support of the people who loved us the way we could if things were normal. To this day, there is a permanent hole in my heart. That void will never be filled, but I have the assurance that I will see her again one day. While I'm here, though, I'm honoring her legacy in every way that I can.

SURVIVING WITH RESILIENCE

Losing my mother has given me a greater appreciation of life and what matters. There were moments when I felt alone because some of the people I thought would reach out didn't. Even in that, God covered us because there were many who did reach out and support us. I started focusing on myself and ways I could become better. I want to be the best woman I can possibly be and the best mother for my two children.

I know God is a keeper. Going through the loss of my marriage and the loss of my mother simultaneously tried to take me out. I became an emotional eater. Recognizing that I have the tendency to isolate and suffer in silence, I knew I needed help. I'm grateful I had and still have a strong support system that includes mentors, counselors, a fitness coach, and a tribe of women who uplifted me. My faith has been through the fire. Yet God has given me peace that has surpassed all understanding. I now effectively co-parent in a way that benefits the children. Our children are in a better space now and thriving. We work together to ensure that both of our children become the best versions of themselves. As for me, I am healing after surviving two life-altering experiences back to back. I am blessed by the elevation and growth resulting from my pain, knowing there is purpose in it all. #ISTILLBELIEVE

God Was Preparing Me: A Mother's Journey of Faith, Love, and Empowerment
Elaine Harris

From the moment of conception, God has a plan for our lives. We may not understand God's purpose as we journey through life until that one day when we have an ah-ha moment.

THE JOURNEY BEGINS
On November 20, 1985, at around 8:00 p.m., I gave birth to a 7-pound, 11-ounce sweet baby boy named Devin. Little did I know God had a unique plan for his life and that this journey would be a testament to His faithfulness and power. Unexpected circumstances marked Devin's birth, despite a normal pregnancy, with monthly doctor visits. There were no signs of difficulty, although 37 years ago, the technology was not like today. Devin made a grand entrance at birth as he hurried into this world. He couldn't wait for his father, Henry, who was on his way to the hospital. He came into this world within five minutes of my arrival at the hospital. The doctors said his birth was precipitous. While in the delivery room, I heard the physician delivering him call out for help. I am not sure, but I believe they dropped him. Devin had a slight cleft palate, dilated pupil, bent index finger, and thumb.

While in the hospital, he was losing weight and would not eat. The nurse gave me cans of formula. Just before discharge, the nurse in the nursery noticed he continued to lose weight. Although I wanted to nurse him, she provided me with cases of formula.; the hospital encouraged me to nurse, but he had problems sucking once we were home. He would not eat, and his diapers were always dry. I immediately took him back to the hospital. I was told he may have died from dehydration if I had not brought him in. I learned just after admission that he had a slight bleed on his brain that could have been caused by the fall or the dehydration. Looking back, he may have been dehydrated before his discharge after birth.

For reasons unknown, the hospital was very supportive, providing me with a private suite and a patient advocate to visit me daily, even providing me with an electric feeding pump and formula when I returned home. With feelings of the unknown, I prayed my baby would be OK. "But I trust in you Lord: I say, 'You are my God My times are in your hands'" (Psalm 31:14–15a NIV).

THE MEDICAL JOURNEY BEGINS

The local children's hospital provided Devin's initial medical care, followed by every department: Genetics, Orthopedics, Neurology, and Ear Nose and Throat (ENT). Genetics gave the diagnosis. With Catel Matzke Syndrome, Devin has something every one in one hundred thousand children has. He was the one in one thousand God sent me to care for. As I share this story, I remember every detail as if it were today. On one of his prior doctor visits, the neurologist told me they did not expect my baby to live a year. This was the second time a physician had said such a horrible thing to me. I knew better, but those words hurt. Upset and crying, I started praying and believing God would make away. "I shall not die, but live, and declare the works of the Lord" (Psalm 118:17 NKJV). This was a devastating thing to hear. I did not expect the baby that I carried for nine months to live. "Children are a gift from the Lord" (Psalm 127:3 NLT). I prayed, and the Lord told me He chose me to believe that He would not take my son from me. I could not understand when he was born, but it quickly became apparent that Devin was a gift from God, and He chose me to love and provide him with care.

As a young African American mother, I felt the impact of disparities in health care receiving the status quo for services. I was not provided with the care that individuals of other ethnicities received. It was my perception, but often, perception is reality. As I reflect, I was never encouraged to attend any support groups with parents with children with disabilities to allow me to share my feelings. But God, I had the love and support of my family and my church family. I left no stone unturned when caring for my baby boy.

After prayer, I decided to take Devin to Temple University Shriners Hospital for his monthly visits. And now Kennedy Kreger in Baltimore, Maryland.

FAMILY LIFE

While providing care for Devin, I could not forget that I had two other children, and as their mother, I had to offer them the same love and support, time, and attention. Providing balance. Soon after the birth of my third child, my husband, Henry, suggested I find someone to come to our home and care for them instead of me taking them out of the house for childcare. God sent me an angel in a matter of a day, a retired neonatal nurse from an area hospital. She became the surrogate mother and grandmother to my children. I could depend on her for everything and constantly don't know what I would have done *without her*. I recognized he was left out of activities, so I began researching programs and activities. I found an away camp in the Maryland Catoctin Mountains adjoined to Camp David; Camp Greentop. This was perfect. I was able to provide him with something that would offer him fun with individuals with disabilities while providing me with respite, in addition to having a loving mother-in-law who would take him and her other grandchildren for the summer.

UNRAVELING SUPPRESSED FEELINGS

It was not until recently that I was able to reflect on my feelings that have been suppressed. From the day Devin was born, my sole purpose was to provide him with love, care, and advocacy, leaving no stone unturned. I felt like the energizer bunny that keeps going and going. I questioned myself, wondering if I had done something wrong. *Am I able to have another child without disabilities? What are people saying about me? What are you looking at? Stop staring at us.* Questions without answers and feelings without end in sight filled my mind and heart. I believed no one could relate to my situation. Although I had love and support, I still felt alone, unable to express my fears and anxiety. Who would understand my feelings and what I was going through? I was made to be strong and withstand adversity. Yet, I still felt as if I was on an island alone. I could not let anyone see me break, with feelings of being left out because I had a disabled child.

A few months after his birth, I worked with individuals who were homeless and mentally ill. I was asked a question during one of the sessions with the company psychiatrist ... I had just received a call from Devin's physician. I did not feel like interacting with anyone—my response was short. After the session, the doctor said it was okay to feel depressed. It was okay to recognize I needed help. All too often, we don't address our feelings of low self-worth and low self-esteem, putting on a mask and putting on a facade, not letting our true feelings come out. It was not until recently when I had a conversation with a young lady with a child born with disabilities that I could see I was not alone in my feelings. Although I was there to help her, little did she realize we were helping each other. My feelings of 37 years ago are the same as her feelings today. We never know the cards we will be dealt in life, but we must play the hand to win. And that is precisely what I have done and will continue to do as long as I have breath to ensure Devin receives the best life offers while I continue working on myself to remove the psychological and remaining emotions.

EDUCATIONAL JOURNEY

Devin was fortunate to be enrolled in the early childhood learning program in Prince George's County, which provided him with programs and services to enhance his development. However, it, too, was met with challenges. Devin's inability to speak clearly could have been enhanced through speech and language services; his approximation of words is excellent, but you would have to know him to understand him. The lack of speech services within the county was a challenge. I constantly sought ways to improve it. I sought assistive technology, which would help my son communicate better. The device he received had simple things like his name, address, and mother and father's contact information. Upon review of the device one day, we heard the teacher's voice say, "My name is Devin Harris, and I am stupid." My head spun, and I immediately contacted the school for an explanation. I had to continuously challenge Individualized Education Plan (IEP) goals to ensure they consistently developed and created new plans to further his growth. I discussed the concept of inclusion within the school system integrating individuals with special needs with the general school population with the local school board representative. My feeling within that meeting was that children are cruel and have the tendency to mistreat individuals with disabilities unintentionally. I was not going to allow that. Not with my son! I knew he was much more than the disability he was born with. I'm proud to say Devin achieved Special Olympics medals in swimming and other activities throughout his education. He was also a Make-a-Wish Foundation awardee and was given a one-day trip to Disney World.

MY SPIRITUAL JOURNEY

Soon after Devin's birth, I had conversations with my spiritual father, Bishop Alfred Owens, Jr., who saw that I needed spiritual support. He appointed me to the Associate Missionary Board, a group of spirit-filled young women who loved the Lord. This appointment strengthened my faith in God and gave me the strength and support to continue my journey. I grew in my walk with the Lord through biblical teachings, prayer, fasting, women's retreats to Brice Mountain, and the feeling of the Holy Ghost. I even received an award for my faith from the Associate Missionary Board.

Although the doctor did not believe my child would live and not die, I stood on God's promise. "Now faith is the substance of things hoped for, the evidence of things not seen" (Hebrews 11:1 KJV).

REFLECTION

Never in a million years would I have imagined having a child with disabilities. Or that I would tell my story, but as I reflect on my life, there was a young lady who lived in my community as a child who was my friend; she was deaf. She stayed in the house to herself. I would play with dolls and jacks with her. I even took her to the skating rink with me. The love and compassion I had and the friendship we had were terrific. The ah-ha moment in God's plan was that He knew my love and compassion for her. Although I moved away from the community, she was always on my mind, always thinking of ways that would enhance her quality of life. Devin and the young lady could not communicate their needs with developmental disabilities; separated from others. Both have gentle, kind, and loving spirits, despite their challenges.

Devin and my former neighbor were all part of God's plan for my life. The Lord never does anything by accident. My first position as a social worker was at a facility in Northern Virginia that cared for children with disabilities. These individuals were treated less than humans and placed in padded rooms with tabasco sauce squirted on open wounds. When showering African American little girls, they hosed them down like animals. This treatment did not sit well in my spirit. I questioned why and provided support and advocacy. One little girl even called me mommy.

I have always had my heart on my sleeve and could not hide my feelings toward any type of injustice. I always treat people with dignity and respect. A few weeks into the job, I was told I was not the right fit. I did not realize that God was watching me. The love and compassion I had for those children would serve me well. Four years later, I gave birth to my son. I consider myself blessed; the Lord chose me. It is my prayer that I can provide support to others with children that are facing challenges. I want you to know that you don't have to walk this journey alone.

WHERE DO WE GO FROM HERE?

We are at year 37. Can God? Yes, He can. Man does not know the God I serve. Through my faith and continued prayer, we have made it. As long as I have breath in my body, I will continue to provide love, care, support, and advocacy for my son with the help and support of my husband, children, and family. The doctors are amazed, and as the doctors said to me 37 years ago, to let him live his life to the fullest is precisely what we intend to do. Yes, we are protective, but that is OK. I am unsure if you are aware, but once a child with disabilities reaches the age of 18, they are considered an adult to make health care or financial decisions. Guardianship is needed for the day you will be unable to provide care. If you can no longer make decisions, identify someone you know who will give the same love and support.

Provide a complete list of medical diagnoses, doctors, and appointments, including phone numbers. Have necessary documentation, birth certificate, non-driver ID, Supplemental Nutrition Assistance Program (SNAP), and Metro Access transportation information. Make sure that there will be continued resources and services available—identify resources to assist others with as they embark upon their journey to provide care in your absence. Identify day programs and away camps to provide respite and contact State and local governments and nonprofit agencies to identify support services and programs. There are resources out there; the key is locating them.

CONCLUSION

Know that God will never leave nor forsake you; He always has your back. Again, we may not initially know God's plan for our life, but know He saw something in you and knew that He built you to handle challenges and adversity and provide the unconditional love your child needs. The journey is far from over, but I know God will be by my side. To know Devin is to love Him. He's always willing to give a helping hand to others; He loves the Lord and continuously gives Him praise.

Although the doctor did not believe my child would live, I stood on God's promise and applied my faith. I believed God's Word then, and I still believe it now. "Now faith is the substance of things hoped for, the evidence of things not seen" (Hebrews 11:1 KJV).

A Heart of Victory!
Priscilla Ademola

Amazing grace, how sweet the sound that saved a wretch like me.[6] I once was lost, but now I am found. I am found because I have Jesus in my life. I was raised in Suriname, officially the Republic of Suriname, a country in northern South America. It is bordered by the Atlantic Ocean to the north, French Guiana to the east, Guyana to the west, and Brazil to the south.

My junior sister and I were raised mostly by my mother because my father never had time for us. While he took care of us, he never spent time with us. I know he loved us, but he didn't express that love. My father never told me he loved me. My parents' marriage had many issues, because my father was cheating. There were many quarrels in the home, and sometimes the argument got out of hand. Our house was small and old. When it rained, water came in freely, and all kinds of creepy crawling animals found their way in. Despite what we went through, we were still happy. However, it was really nice to not have outside water and animals inside with us.

My mother decided to go to the Netherlands because she finally had enough of my father's cheating. He thought my mother was going on holiday. In fact, my mother never returned to my father. My sister and I went to live with my grandmother for two years. A lot happened in my life in those two years. My uncle, a voodoo ritualist, sexually abused me several times. He had a special room with all kinds of statues and images that he worshipped. People visited my uncle's house for readings and spiritual baths for protection. Like the people who came to see my uncle, I used to believe in the rituals and readings. My family was deeply rooted in voodoo practice. Praise God, many of my family are converted and are Christians now.

---

[6]https://library.timelesstruths.org/music/Amazing_Grace/

Back to the stories about my uncle sexually assaulting me; I was 14 when the abuse started. He called me into his room because he said he wanted to do a reading for me. While in the room, he began touching me, I tried to push him away, but I couldn't. There was some kind of evil power that came over him. You can imagine how scared I was as a child. My uncle told me not to tell anyone; otherwise, I would die. Now that I think back, I was just being manipulated.

My uncle abused me several times in multiple places, including his garden. I also remember being assaulted in the middle of a forest. We were away with the family for a few days. It was where all kinds of rituals took place, including the evening dance to worship the gods. During this dance, we go into a trance, and the spirits take possession of our bodies. This ceremony is part of winti, an animalistic religion practiced mainly by Surinamese Creoles. That night, my uncle took me to the forest. He said he had to do something for me. It was in the middle of the night, after 12 midnight. My family did not say anything because they thought my uncle had to do ritual things for me. My uncle took advantage of the situation. He just wanted to perform sexual acts on me.

My uncle had such power over the family that he fought us spiritually with his evil spirits when we came to Christ. He lived right next to my grandmother. Looking out the window as I did the dishes in my grandmother's kitchen, I could also see my uncle in his kitchen. I didn't like it when we made eye contact. I didn't like that at all. I always closed the curtain when I saw him in the kitchen. He once asked me why I was hiding behind that curtain. I didn't have an answer. He then said that if I continued hiding, people would suspect something. I couldn't understand how my uncle could do that to me. My uncle was supposed to protect me; instead, he sexually abused me. My uncle sexually abused several women of different ages; he was a pedophile.

One day, my uncle was arrested, but after a few days, he was out of jail. He used that evil power to get himself out of jail. The police had gone to his home to check the room where he was abusing the women; what I heard was that the police could not get access to that haunted room. At some point, I started having boyfriends at the age of 14. Many people started gossiping about me, and some said I had HIV because I had become very thin. The spirit of lust was in control of me. I had boyfriends here and didn't care about my life then. It was a pleasure when a man told me I was beautiful. I started to dress very provocatively, dressed to kill. I remember being in a relationship with a man much older than me. I once went to a hotel with him and stayed late at night. My family worried about me because they didn't know where I was.

One night when I came home late, I was beaten by my aunt. My family became increasingly angry with me. That evening, they took me to the police station to report the beating. I was sad that my ex was arrested because of me. As I write this, the Lord instructed me to reach out to him and ask him to forgive me for the trouble I caused. Thankfully, he said he had forgiven me when I spoke to him. He was shocked that I had contacted him. When the Lord gives us instructions, we must obey. I found it difficult to call my ex because I didn't know how he would react, so I humbled myself and got in touch. I thank the Lord for giving me the grace to ask for forgiveness.

My mother visited my sister and me during the two years we lived with my grandmother, as our visa to the Netherlands had been rejected several times. My mother was shocked when she saw me. I had become very skinny. Because she didn't understand why I was so thin, and I couldn't tell her what was going on, she took me to be examined by a doctor.

Finally, my sister and I could leave for Holland after two years. It was the best day of my life; finally reunited with my mother. I was allowed to start school one week after we arrived in the Netherlands. One day at school, something happened, and I burst into tears. My teacher asked me what had happened, and I told him about the sexual abuse. He immediately made me talk to a trusted person from school. I had two conversations with a social worker, and I was told to tell my mother what had happened to me. I had decided it was easier to write my mother a letter. She was shocked by what had taken place. My mother confronted my uncle, and he admitted what he had done. As a family, we decided not to make a police case out of it.

In Holland, I started dating. I had a wild lifestyle and didn't care about my life. I didn't see my worth, was insecure, and was disgusted with myself. Sometime later, I met my husband through a cousin. My husband told me he immediately knew I would be his wife when he saw me. I asked him what he saw in me because I was so wild. He said to me that I looked tough on the outside, but he knew I was a different person on the inside. My husband was a believer. Although he was backslidden, I often saw him pray and read the Bible. I never showed any interest.

In 2007, while in Amsterdam, I went to church with my aunt. I sat in the last seat, wearing dark sunglasses to hide. I was also pregnant with my first son. The pastor asked who wanted to give his/her life to Jesus. At that moment, I heard two voices in my head saying yes and no. Suddenly, a woman approached me and said, "You want to accept the Lord, but you have doubts." She continued speaking, saying, "Today is your day to give your life to the Lord." With certainty, I can say that was the best decision I ever made in my life.

Before my new birth, many of my family members and I believed in spiritual doctors. But God orchestrated a situation for a change in my family history. One of my mother's sisters was diagnosed with cancer. We thought the spiritual doctors, including my uncle, could help her, but they couldn't. My aunt passed away, but Glory to God, she gave her life to Christ before she died. My aunt's death was a wake-up call for us. We realized that spiritual doctors cannot heal anybody. God is the healer. I am proud to say that many of my family members gave their lives to Christ. I really thank God that we are safe through His blood.

After giving my life to Jesus, I started attending church. I had many questions as a new believer. For instance, I wondered if I could still party or listen to 'worldly' music. How was I supposed to dress? My inquiring mind wanted to know. I realized that the closer I became to the Lord, the less interest I had in things of the world. I am reminded of James 4:8, which says, "Draw near to God, and He will draw near to you. Cleanse your hands, you sinners, and purify your hearts, you double-minded." (NKJV)

After giving birth to our first son, I married at 22. I never considered marrying or becoming something good in society, but God had decided otherwise. I did not know that God had big plans for my life. Yes, He has plans according to Jeremiah 29:11 (NLT), "For I know the plans I have for you, says the Lord. They are plans for good and not for disaster, to give you a future and a hope." I understand now that since birth, the devil wanted to take my life. He tried to destroy me, but the Lord said it shall not be so. The Bible says in John 10:10, "The thief cometh not, but for to steal, and to kill, and to destroy: I have come that they might have life, and that they might have it more abundantly." (KJV) God gave me life abundantly.

As my journey with the Lord continues, I have learned about forgiveness. I forgave my uncle, or at least I thought I had until God put a song on my heart to minister in dance. It is called "A Heart that Forgives." The Lord told me, "Before you minister through this song, you must first call your uncle to say you have forgiven him."

Believe me, I did not find it easy to take the step to call him, but I obeyed. I called him, and I said to him, "I am a believer. I have given my life to Jesus and learned to forgive. I forgive you for what you did to me."

He told me he would ask God to forgive him, and I told him, "I love you with the love of the Lord." I guess he was surprised when I said that. When I forgave him, a burden left me, and things started moving in my life to the glory of God. The Bible says in Mark 11:25, "And whenever you stand praying if you have anything against anyone, forgive him, that your Father in heaven may also forgive you your trespasses." (NKJV) I want to share with everyone that no matter what people do to you, forgive them. If you don't forgive, you live in pain, bitterness, and hatred. Believe me, the person who hurt you will just move on with her or his life. Forgive so that you may have peace in your heart.

In 2019, I moved back to Suriname with my family. I met my uncle and hugged him. My uncle commented that I had become fat. I told him that I had lost some weight, and he asked if losing weight looked like this. I didn't like what he said; it hurt me. Certain thoughts came up in me, like *Why did I forgive him?* I rebuked those thoughts immediately. The Bible, in Matthew 18:21–22, says, "Lord, how often shall my brother sin against me, and I forgive him? Up to seven times?" Jesus said to him, "I do not say to you, up to seven times, but up to seventy times seven." (NKJV) People can hurt us repeatedly, but we must have a heart to forgive. I heard a preacher say she has decided to forgive people in advance so that forgiveness comes immediately when someone hurts her. When you forgive, the healing process starts. Many people find it difficult to forgive. They look at the pain inflicted on them, making it difficult to let go.

In 2016, the Lord revealed to me why I didn't want to socialize with people and kept them at a distance. The sexual abuse inflicted on me by my uncle had a big impact on my life. Hiding from him caused me to hide and disassociate from people. I never wanted to go if someone wanted to meet me for a drink. I would have nice conversations over the phone, but I didn't want to meet. I still have trouble meeting up, but I'm open to it now. I can remember when the Lord gave me an assignment where I had to meet with the women of our church congregation one-on-one. Only because I wanted to obey God was I able to overcome my hesitancy.

What we have gone through in our lives can have so much impact. Because of my testimony, I have met many women who find forgiveness difficult. By God's grace, I could take them through the process of forgiving with prayer. I always say, "Don't get stuck and hang on to the pain of what the person has done to you. Holding on to that pain hurts you, not them." Forgiveness is a process; not everyone can forgive immediately. Some of the women I counseled needed time to forgive, and that's okay. I always say God's grace is sufficient. If you have forgiven the person, it doesn't mean you let the person back into your life. Sometimes that happens; praise God, but if it doesn't, praise God. The Bible says in 1 Thessalonians 5:18 to, "Give thanks in all circumstances; for this is God's will for you in Christ Jesus." (NIV)

Not forgiving can affect our mental and physical health. A testimony that has stuck with me: a lady had been abused by her sister's husband, resulting in her becoming pregnant. Her son did not know about the details of his birth or who his father was. Because of that situation, that lady could not relate to her son. After hearing me testify, she boldly told her son about what happened in her past. Her son cried. He said he had a feeling that something was not right with his mother. She is completely relieved and free by telling her secret to her son. As a result, he has promised that he will do his best to improve his life.

Being able to forgive makes me feel so free. An OVERCOMER! When the thoughts come back about what my uncle did to me, believe me, it doesn't hurt anymore. It seems like it didn't even happen. The Lord has completely healed me from the pain of thoughts would surface. I wondered why I forgave the man that hurt me so badly. I learned to rebuke those thoughts. I said loudly, "I FORGIVE MY UNCLE!" I overcame it.

I pray that we will all have a heart that forgives. A heart that lets go of bitterness, hatred, resentment, anger, and hurt. The Lord said to me once, "When you are humble, you will forgive." I pray that we will have a humble heart to forgive.

Just Because It Is Destined Doesn't Mean It Will Be Easy
Dr. Aikyna Finch

We all know we are destined for something as we look over our lives. No matter what it was, when it finally happened, we realized that things in our life prepared us for that destined moment or thing. We have all had those moments when we tried to do our own thing or go our own way. Still, we failed every time until we yielded to the will of God and did it the way He laid out the path for it to happen, and then, like magic, you win. The destined moment that I was being prepared for was the moment I realized I was going into ministry, the journey that led to today, my journey into ministry.

As a child, I thought ministry was a badge of honor and that all the ministers I knew were powerful and stood in their authority. I was always fascinated, unaware of where my destiny would lead me. In my teenage years and 20s, I was in and out of church due to hurt and fear of the things that were stirring inside me. All of my religious actions ceased because of the fear of the unknown. People spend more time worrying about what they can't see instead of asking the Lord for the answers. Just know that He may not answer when you want, but He always responds in perfect time. I wish I had learned this earlier because I would have been much further now. I am learning now that it wasn't my time to understand those things because I wasn't equipped to handle what came with that life.

By 29, I was at a different church, had accepted the call on my life, and was part of an all-woman associate minister's team. One of us was licensed by our pastor, but the other two weren't. Here it is. God revealed to me that I would be a minister, and I accepted. I had the initial sermon and was given the title Evangelist. I preached on a regular rotation and did all the minister's duties. But I didn't fully understand what I had said YES to. I was living in a land of rose petals and moonbeams because only the glitter had been explained to me, but I soon found out what exactly came with the call.

During my time there, I served, learned, and was dedicated. However, I was disappointed when I left for a job opportunity in another state and was given a certificate of appreciation for my years of hard work. When I asked about my license, I was told by the pastor that God didn't tell him to license me. I didn't step foot in a church after that for years. How could this be? I discovered later that it had something to do with the perceived belief that my doctoral studies were taking me away from my church duties. I wasn't serious in the pastor's eyes because I didn't choose church above all else. What I took from that situation was that I was not about to apologize to a man for being a woman and for wanting to better myself. It wasn't going to happen. Now that I have had time to think about the situation, the Lord probably didn't tell him to license me because it wasn't time yet. I needed to go through more in life before I could be the minister that God needed me to be.

About three years later, I found another church that made me feel welcome and was ready to try again. I started working, and everything was good. Then I approached the pastor about my ministry. He asked for the contact information of my former pastor, and the former pastor sent a letter about my past service. There was a copy in the package for me. When I read it, I had a rush of every emotion at once, but they all quickly turned to anger. After he said everything, he ended with this sentence, "When she decides to dedicate herself to ministry, she will be a powerful preacher."

It was just another dagger in my heart to me. I was determined after that. I served, but sadly, I left that ministry again without my license. It would be a few years before I would find a new church I felt comfortable serving in. I had to work to fulfill my calling. I had to study, not only to show myself approved. I had to travel the course laid out for me by God. I was knocked off the path whenever I was defiant or pushed back. But I would eventually dust myself off and get back on track for Him to put me right back into a situation to learn the lesson I was supposed to learn in the first place.

In 2014, I met a person that would change my life. I would come home to visit my mother in Nashville, and like clockwork, this woman named Jewell Marie Grandberry would show up at her house. She would always greet me, "Hello, woman of God." It would ring in my ears. I attempted to hide when she came over, but she would always be there. After we had played this game for a few years, I was summoned to the church. There she sat on the pew, waiting for me. She said, "So, are you done playing yet? What are you going to do?" We had a conversation, which made me think about my ministry again.

In 2015, I lost my grandmother, and my friend got married, so it made sense to move back home because I was spending so much time driving back and forth. The tug to return to church got stronger after I moved home. I started to attend church off and on with my mother. During this time, my educational and tech careers blossomed simultaneously. I continued to be pulled toward ministry, even though it was a busy time in my life.

During New Year's Eve Service in 2016, I joined the church. I enjoyed learning with two other ministers in training. Sadly, it ended in hurt like the rest of the churches. It was not the pastor this time. It was other people, but the pastor didn't rescue me. She let me go along my merry way. I didn't understand it then, but she couldn't intervene because I had to travel this journey of my free will. I didn't go back to church for years after that.

In 2019, I felt the need to go to her Pastor's Anniversary. The speaker said, "You need a leader who is unafraid to cut you." I understood then why I had to be there. It was time to come back. This was different because I had never returned to a place of hurt before. Especially not for more of what I perceived as abuse. Had I lost my mind? In January 2020, I joined that church again and returned to pick up where I left off. But the part I will never forget that made me know the Lord will put you back on the destined path is when I stepped into my first minister's meeting since my return. Who was sitting next to me? The same minister in training that started with me in 2017.

I started back on the path to licensing, but because of Covid-19, the process went from July 2020 to July 2022. During that time, I preached my first sermon at the church in August 2020, and from there, I was added to the preaching, teaching, and worship leader rotation. I started to learn the ways of the organization and the rules of order as a minister. Much of it was familiar, but some of it was new. I enjoyed the learning piece because I love a good learning moment as a professor. I started to notice different gifts emerging that I had not used in a long time, but this time, they were stronger. Once, I went to the altar for prayer, and the pastor had the prophet of the church pray for me. He made a statement about the journey I had ahead. Then the pastor told me, "You know you have the gift, and if I be a woman of God, you will be all you are supposed to be before I leave this earth." It was quiet because everyone knew what that meant, so when the service was over, people came to me to comment on what was said after the prayer.

After that, I knew I had to learn how to handle and explore my gifts to learn more about myself. The one thing I know about myself is that I learn by doing, so I had to find a way to explore my gifts and talents. I found my outlet on the Clubhouse app. Getting up at 6:30 a.m. Sunday–Friday to share and celebrate God's promises was important to my development as a minister. I felt free to develop and grow in that space. To this day, it is still serving as a learning environment in my life. I discovered that my emotions trigger my gifts, so I am learning to control them to grow in them.

My bishop tried to get the board to review us, the ministers in training, in 2020 and 2021, but that didn't work out. I was in a season of learning about God's timing vs. my own. It was something that I had always struggled with, but I was getting a crash course in patience. I wanted my license since 2008 and felt I earned it, but yet, it seemed that since then, it had always eluded me. I see now that I needed to learn some things to hold the mantle that God has placed on my life. Usually, when I didn't get my way, I would leave, but this time, something inside me told me to finish the journey. I knew I had to be close with all the spiritual warfare happening around the license, so I decided to see it through to the end.

In March 2022, we started preparing for Congress, our denomination's equivalent of a National Convention. All of a sudden, time started moving very fast. Airfare, hotel, registration, license testing prep, and buying five days of white outfits seemed to happen simultaneously. My mom, determined to see me become a licensed minister even though she was suffering from complications of a mastectomy, traveled with me in July 2022 to Michigan. Caring for my mother while we were in Michigan helped me to see that part of my journey was to serve my mom as a nurse. I know now that everything that happens in life has a reason and purpose.

We were pulled out of the minister's class on Monday after arrival, bright and early, to go to the examining board. Eight of us from various regions in the country went up for licensing. We were the last group, so we had to wait and sit in our nervousness. Thankfully, the group was able to go in together. I was chosen to give the message. It was the first time someone asked to hear my preacher's voice. I knew that my voice changed when I preached, but I had never thought about being able to call it up on demand. I was shocked by that revelation. After the licensing process, I was the last to pay my fee. I answered the final question by quoting John 3:16 in my preacher's voice. It was a weird feeling to be able to switch to a preaching voice in an instant. I took it as a sign of growth.

Each day, I went to classes and workshops. My favorite was the prophecy class. I realized I had questions in all the classes and was behind in several areas. That was uncomfortable because I don't feel that way about learning very often. My bishop picked people to represent different areas, but I was not chosen. This allowed me to learn about Congress and how it worked. Eventually, I ended up with the Technology Team; imagine that. They were so welcoming. I love being in that atmosphere because it helped me connect with my ministerial side. I realize I have much to learn and must approach ministry differently. You can't navigate a God thing like you would a man thing. The rules and motivations are different, and you must be open and teachable to develop into the person you are supposed to be for the Kingdom.

On that Friday of the Congress, in July 2022, I received my license. I finally held that piece of paper I had wanted for so long. I can say that it was an amazing day. My mom made her attempt at recording the momentous milestone. Of course, I had a backup recording, but she did try. Thanks, Mom!

As I was standing in the receiving line after the service, I realized that the license was just the beginning of a new journey. The first journey got to the lock, and the next journey gave me the key. The last part of this walk after ordination will let me unlock the door to my whole self. I am excited to meet her and see all she has to offer the Kingdom.

After all the difficulties, I followed God's destined path for me, despite the obstacles, including myself. I now have the wisdom to see my part in the journey, good and bad. Shifting blame never helped anyone in the situation. Facing the truth for what it is and growing from it always does. At the end of the day, everything I went through brought me to today. I have a leader that believes in my ministry and my gifts and supports me. I am surrounded by supportive women preachers who understand my struggle because they have survived their own. I have learned to appreciate my journey and where it will take me. Ministry no longer means pain and trials; it now means standing despite what you have gone through because your journey was worth the testimony so you can let others know about the miracles God can perform for them.

Rejected. Protected. Perfected
Michelle Clark

Rejection is the sense of being unwanted and unable to receive love from others. As early as two years old, I remember being molested by my aunt, who was supposed to take care of me when my mother went to work. She would position me on her body so that I would have to suck her breast and dry hump her. I think the abuse stopped right before I started kindergarten. At this young age, I thought it meant she didn't love me anymore. It was my first feeling of rejection, even though I didn't know the proper name for the emotion. I felt unloved and unwanted. I also believed terrible things would happen if my aunt couldn't care for me while my mom worked. My pre-k brain didn't understand that bad things were happening.

I felt rejected in many areas of my life. Never knowing my biological father left me feeling like something was missing, a hole that couldn't be filled. There were missing puzzle pieces of my identity. I knew I was a Clark. I knew that Caroline was my mother. I knew I had all these aunts and uncles on my mom's side of the family. However, a piece of me was still missing. It needed to come from my biological father. It is something I have never had and still want.

Dealing with rejection growing up was not easy. It fosters a lack of trust, even when it comes to family. I was suspicious of everybody and had faith in very few people. As a result, it was difficult for me to date because the trust factor would always come into play. It didn't help that my mother always shied away from giving me many details about my biological father.

Trust me, I'm not blaming her for not wanting to tell me or perhaps for not knowing who he was. Maybe she knew and never told him he had a daughter. Perhaps she told him, and he didn't want the responsibility of raising me. I simply do not know. She had reasons, whether I understood them or not. So, there was always a part of me as a child that needed reassurance, validation, and love from male figures. I was trying to replace what I didn't get from my father, even though my uncles on my mom's side were good to me. Yet, that spirit followed me around through my teens.

My mom married later on in life. However, I never had a close relationship with my stepfather. As a young child, I saw things in him and knew I could not trust him. My instincts about him were not wrong. He proved it during my teenage years. He was physically and verbally abusive to my mother. Witnessing him abuse my mother caused me to put up even more walls. Each time I saw him hit her or denigrate her, I told myself, *Michelle, this is why you can never trust men.* Even when I wanted to put my trust in a guy, I would withdraw behind my walls. I thought they were my safe space, especially since I held the key. Absolutely no one could come in and rob me of my peace.

The early childhood molestation I suffered caused me to struggle as an adult. The same aunt who defiled me as a toddler gave a deathbed confession as I gave birth to my oldest daughter, Danielle. She was dying of breast cancer at the time. On her sickbed, as if she was recounting the horrors of what she had done to me, my aunt asked if she had molested me. It seemed like all her demons were coming for her before she passed over to the other side. I answered, "Yes, you did." At that moment, she asked for my forgiveness. I told her she was forgiven and that I had carried a lot of guilt. I thought it was my fault for what she had done. I didn't understand why she did it or chose me to be her victim.

The one bright light was my faith. Despite what I went through, it's all I had to hold onto. I may not have trusted people, but I knew I could trust God. In Him, I found a place of peace. I found safety and sanity. When I shared what my aunt did, my family didn't believe me. I grew up in an era where such things were not shared. There was the belief that a closed mouth is always better than exposing the demons and darkness in many families. It's the old notion that whatever goes on in this house should stay in this house and not talk about it. Generations suffer because no one will believe those who speak up. But, even through all that trauma, I never cursed God. I hung on to Him for dear life because He was the only way I could survive.

I still give God all the glory, knowing I'm still here for a reason. God kept me for a purpose that is beyond my understanding. I'm slowly trying to get to the point of learning my purpose. Perhaps it was to share my story so another sister could be free. I am sure I am not the only child to have been mishandled by a trusted family member. I know other girls were not believed. I know other girls were looked down on and thought of as being fast or even tempting the abuser. I'm still here to tell some sister that deliverance, restoration, and being whole is possible.

I have learned that you can't have a closed eye or closed mouth. You must always tell the truth and literally shame the devil. You can never be free otherwise and walk in true deliverance. There came a time when I had to walk in total forgiveness of everyone I thought participated in what happened to me as a child. I had to forgive my mom for never telling me who my biological father was, no matter her reasons. As I stated earlier, I forgave my aunt for doing what she did to me because mental illness is real. You had to have been mentally ill to molest a toddler. Sadly, mental illness is not always discussed, especially in black families.

I forgave my stepfather. Even though I'm not married, I know that marriage is not always easy. It can be tough to break toxic mindsets and behaviors passed down from generation to generation. I understand that if you never get healed from past hurts or deal with your issues, you will carry them into your new relationship. I also know that forgiveness is a lot easier said than done. You must have a hard talk with yourself and never leave Jesus out of the conversation because forgiveness is not for the other person. Forgiveness is definitely for you. The longer you hold on to stuff, the longer it will take you to reach your next level. So, I forgave.

I had a mindset to forgive and still love, despite certain people not loving me back, but I had to get free. I had to get free from having a wall up. The walls I put up were for protection and did not include Jesus. They had to come down if I was going to experience freedom as God intended it. I had to get free from the emotional trauma of being molested. Some who've been sexually traumatized suffer identity crises, others struggle with their sexual identity, and others become highly promiscuous. For me, it was not letting anyone get close. I believed if I couldn't trust my family to protect me, I couldn't trust anyone else. I had to get free from self-sabotage. God sent people in my life that tried to love me to a place of wholeness. But when your trust meter is on zero and has been shot to hell from a very young age, sometimes you get blinded to those who mean you no harm.

The Scripture that tells us to be transformed by renewing our mind helped me to believe I could have a new mind. (See Romans 12:2) I started to believe I was capable of receiving and giving love. I could trust and be trusted. If someone fell short of my expectations, I couldn't put the walls back up. I had to learn not to internalize it and find fault because everyone is a work in progress, knowing we can all fail the one we love the most. That's where forgiveness comes in. I used to hate myself because I didn't understand why things didn't always work out how I wanted them to.

When relationships would fall apart, I blamed myself until I learned to take a step back and really look at what happened. Seeing clearly, I realized God didn't hate me. Sometimes we were just not compatible; other times, it wasn't about me at all. It was the guy who had issues. When I asked myself why I was going through this again and why He allowed it, I stopped being so upset because I was confident it would all work out for my good. I stopped taking things so personally, even though rejection is a hard pill to swallow. I've often heard people in church say that rejection is God's protection. Let me add that rejection just might be God's protection for perfection.

I might not understand or like it while going through it, but I will always give God glory. What I know for sure is that there is victory on the other side. There is peace on the other side. There is joy, restoration, and wholeness on the other side of rejection. Because if God is for me, He's more than anything or anyone who is against me.

So, I say to you, my sister, you might have been tried in the fire, but you have come out like silver refined and pure gold. You are more than a survivor. You are thriving.

The Day I Decided to Lose It!
Minister Da´Mali Goings

When I first sat to write this chapter, my thoughts were all over the place. I was just coming off a painful experience that caused me to take a second look at my decisions and how I dealt with hurt, offenses, and even speaking up for myself when the evidence of my history did not tell the same story. As you read this chapter, I pray that you will be inspired and encouraged to lose the things that hold you in bondage and dim the light that lives inside of you, which is meant for the world to see and ultimately glorify God.

As a 48-year-old woman, I struggle with losing weight. It has become so exhausting at times, especially since I have many fond memories of primping in the mirror, boasting about how thin I was. These pictures display a curvy but attractive look, and my muscles were very defined through my activeness in sports. My calves were rock hard, proving that I walked in strength and could walk many miles, squat, and carry much weight. The attention from others that I received just affirmed that I was truly that chic, or so I thought.

However, as I aged and had children, I carried emotional and mental baggage. The trauma that my body experienced began to show externally in the form of obesity. I went from being warned that I was overweight and reaching a peak where my Body Mass Index (BMI) would declare that I was obese to being diagnosed on paper as OBESE with an ICD 10 medical billing code that follows me to this day. Once I had my first warning, I went into an internal spinout. I began to see myself as unwell, unattractive, and sad, and the happiest versions of myself became lost and practically died.

Let me pause here by saying that our looks should not be the criteria to determine if we are attractive. It also should not be the thing that alters our own truth about how we really look. The Scripture tells us in 1 Peter 3:4 that beauty "should be that of your inner self, the unfading beauty of a gentle and quiet spirit, which is of great worth in God's sight." (NIV)

When this started to happen to me, I had not been deeply rooted in God's Word and only knew God to be the creator. The Sunday school lessons, Sunday sermon series, and the routine of doing church were all I had as a foundation. Because of this, the image of who I was was destroyed by the words of someone who had no relation to me but was being paid to take care of me.

This played within my life for well over 27 years. During the 27 years, I went through several life-changing, emotionally impacting, mentally agonizing moments that added to the internal weight gain. I walked in pain every day, not physical pain, but the mental and emotional pains that came from having low self-esteem and no longer seeing myself as a beautiful woman but as someone who did not matter.

I recall hitting a breaking point in 1997 when I first encountered the truth about why I was obese. I was sitting in my apartment, having just returned home from a long day at work to my boyfriend and two small children. I had a break. I couldn't take another moment in my life with an unemployed boyfriend. I was tired from working every day at a Chiropractor's office in Virginia, dealing with other patients' problems and health concerns, driving over an hour and a half back home from work, and then coming home where nothing was done. The house needed to be cleaned, dinner needed to be fixed, and I had had enough. So, in a moment of weakness, the tears began to flow, and emotionally I could not stop crying. Looking back on that time, I laugh because I can only imagine what he was thinking about me, but I DID NOT CARE! My mother was called over, and the two of them tried to figure out how to get me to stop crying.

They decided to take me in for an emergency mental health appointment. When I arrived, no one was able to go inside with me. I sat across from a psychiatrist, and he asked me what happened. This was the very first time in my life that I had been completely honest about what was going on in my life and going on with me. I was desperate to find out what was happening to me. When I finished talking through it, the doctor said in the most freeing way possible,

"There is NOTHING WRONG WITH YOU! You just had enough. You are a mom with a 3½-year-old and an 18-month-old. Many mothers go through this. You are going to be okay." Those words were the most liberating words that could have been said to me. I left there with a plan to manage my stress better and learn to say no. I began a journey with talk therapy and one-on-one counseling to get to the root of my problem. All those symptoms and events would lead one to believe the problem was in my home. But it wasn't. It was much deeper than that.

Here are some of the things I identified on my way to losing the weight and burdens of my life in secret, which ultimately impacted my decisions and choices and led me to that emotional break:

- **EVENT #1:** My father and mother separated when I was 12, turning 13, and I began living a life filled with anger, resentment, and secrets. I protected my parents from the results of their failures. I took responsibility for things that happened to me, not allowing the burden and weight of those things to impact anyone else but me. I was left having to take care of my two younger brothers, and, at times, I took care of my mother, who was mentally and emotionally unable to manage during the first four years of their separation. My mom worked late nights and spent most of her days working overtime. She even worked a part-time job just to make ends meet. My father was absent most of that time. I only saw him when I sought him out. Although I remained hopeful that my father would get himself together and come home, this hope also hurt my mother even more, causing a humungous disconnect. Basically, I had been neglected.

- **Event #2:** When I turned 13 years old, I made a bad decision to skip school and go with a good friend to her boyfriend's house. There, her friend's uncle had just newly been released from prison and found his next victim in me, seizing the opportunity to sexually assault me while they were in another room. I left there without telling one person. Instead, I went home, spray painted his name in my closet just in case something was wrong with me because of what he did, and then went on with my life, not realizing because of my age that I was stifling my voice even more. My personality changed, and I was fighting internal depression, all while physically fighting everyone else. I felt that no one saw me and no one was coming to rescue me from the deep hole I was falling into. I was weighted down.

- **Event #3:** Having been raised by a single mother who was struggling mentally and emotionally with her issues impacted my life severely and taught me incorrectly how to deal with traumatic life-altering events. I learned the wrong coping skills. I could not build a solid maternal relationship with my mother, which caused me to desire a certain type of love that could never be experienced with anyone else. This left a gaping hole in my soul, and I looked to other things to fill its place but instead chose people with a personality like my mother to gain their approval. Ultimately, this was a massive failure and hurt me even greater the older I got. This added more weight to my life.

These things were complicated because they involved people I loved and cared for. Besides, no one wants to admit that their parents neglected them at various times. As I write this, I am trying to find ways to still honor both of my parents so that their shortcomings, mistakes, and weaknesses will not outweigh their achievements and accomplishments that positively impacted my life. As a daughter, it hurt me to realize that their lack of presence in my life hurt me tremendously. It had a major impact on my choices and self-esteem as a young woman. It impacted who I chose as a husband and ultimately was the foundation of why I stayed in a toxic relationship. Until I was 35, I lived a life filled with brokenness, pain, and unresolved internal issues with my mother and father.

As those years passed, I experienced turmoil, toxicity from the ending of my marriage, and the weightiness of having to appear perfect without believing or even taking the time to deal with my own wounds. My weight was really a metaphor for the wounds that I had inside and out. It was the evidence that I was suffering in silence. I never talked about my suffering, but my body began speaking loudly.

In 2018, I came back home as an adult. I lived in the same house where I experienced many of the traumatic experiences that molded and shaped my responses and thoughts about life. It was a time when I did not know God was truly doing something major for my mother and for me, especially since she and I did not have a very close relationship bond as mother and daughter. It was not because I did not want one. That was furthest from the truth. I yearned for it and had many moments of sadness, prayers, and conversations with God to fix what was broken in me and between my mother and me. He told me to give away all my stuff and go back home. Take nothing for my journey. He told me to stay for six months so that I could save and purchase my next home. After a little bucking, I obeyed, and my mother said yes. I moved into my old bedroom, the smallest room in the house. Honestly, it felt so awkward; all I wanted to do was run away. It felt as if I was 13 again. But then things shifted drastically. A couple of weeks passed, and my mother took ill. She had complications from a knee replacement surgery a year before and had a staph infection. In the twinkling of an eye, I became my mother's caretaker. This forced us both to become humble and let God deal with our wounds.

She eventually went into a rehab center where she was neglected and was hospitalized for kidney failure due to medications she was taking. The Lord had strengthened me to take on this task of being her advocate. After weeks in the hospital, she returned home only to have a flare-up of the infection again, eventually leading to her passing that following January. During the time that she was home, she apologized to me because she felt that it wasn't fair for me to be the one to have to be there to take care of her. I reassured her that I wanted to be there to care for her and that I was not going anywhere. I kept my promise. I was there up until she took her last breath.

The point of the story is that God has a way of bringing things full circle. I never thought I would lose my mother so soon after moving back home, but I came home just in time to heal and become a grown woman at 45. I am still a work in progress. The wounds are healing in God's timing and not my own. While I am in my healing season, I am continuously staying on my knees. I pray throughout the day, read the Bible, and stay in God's face.

One of the final messages my mother sent me via text before her death was to always speak up for myself and never allow anyone to mistreat me. It was a life-changing text message because it signaled that she did see me and knew what I needed after she was gone. So, if you are reading my chapter, and some, if not all, of these things are relatable to you, and you, too, have a weight (wound) issue, then this prayer is for you:

> Father,
> I pray for healing and deliverance for my dear sister or brother today. May the wounds of their heart be healed. May the tears they shed be dried, and in exchange for the tears, may they receive a supernatural joy that only You can provide. Walk with them daily, even through the toughest battles, and may they decide to lose every weight and cast their cares on You. In Jesus' name, AMEN!

My parting word is that God knows and will respond in due season when you least expect it. He has done it for me and is still doing it now. "Therefore we also, since we are surrounded by so great a cloud of witnesses, let us lay aside every weight, and the sin which so easily ensnares *us,* and let us run with endurance the race that is set before us, [2] looking unto Jesus, the [a]author and [b]finisher of *our* faith, who for the joy that was set before Him endured the cross, despising the shame, and has sat down at the right hand of the throne of God" (Hebrews 12:1–2). (KJV)

A Voice for the Voiceless
LaShaune Lee

You intended to harm me, but God intended it <u>ALL</u> for good. He brought me to this position so I could save the lives of many people. —**Genesis 50:20, NLT (emphasis mine)**

I have never been the type of person that stood out in a crowd— never someone people would naturally gravitate to. Unless you already know me, I don't feel like I command a space when I enter it. And even then, am I commanding the area or just a familiar face? You probably would not even notice me otherwise. I am quiet and unassuming. I do not go for the spotlight; I tend to run from it. I dislike being out front because I don't need the 'fishbowl' experience. The spotlight does not add anything to me, except anxiety.

Nothing about me stands out, nothing that would send vibes like "Hey, you just might want to talk to her. She is your answer." Remember when you cried out to God for help to be delivered from that bondage? You prayed for God to send someone who would understand and not judge you. You prayed for God to send someone who would see you and help you right where you are—that low place, that lonely place, that defeated place. You prayed for someone to help you get from here to there; well … I am that woman. I am learning that I am the answer to someone's prayer. I am the answer to YOUR prayer. What I have endured is not wasted time or effort— the mistakes, the neglect, the abuse, the rejection, the 'you're not good enough,' the false perceptions from people, the hurt, the loneliness, the isolation (I am going to tell you about that one), the tears I cried that nobody but Jesus knows about—not even my husband, and I tell him just about everything! These experiences and this suffering were for **you**! All of it was for the person who would read a story I never thought I would tell—because, honestly, I didn't believe you would care.

Now, for the super deep folks, I am quite aware those thoughts are from the devil. He is real, and he HATES me—just like he hates you. Hate him back! That's what I learned, and I will tell you how I do it. Again, nothing deep: I hate the devil back by living—and living well! And that is not about having everything I want (that hardly ever happens) or everything I need ('cause sometimes the Lord takes entirely too long)! I hate the devil back by SURVIVING! I have come to the realization that I have survived some STUFF! The old me would have chosen another word, and you probably know the word. Sometimes the word occasionally comes out too—yes, I am saved, but I am not perfect. And some things we go through in life will cause us to speak in other tongues that are not holy. I am, and you are, a work in progress. If I am going to tell you my story and show you how to make it, I have to be me. So, some grace, please, and thank you; praise Jesus! Did I tell y'all I'm funny? I really am! I have to laugh to keep from crying—although weeping does not make you 'weak.'

Crying is actually cleansing, and it releases toxins from your system. Other health benefits come from having a good cry, such as releasing stress and emotional pain. Crying is a 'safety valve' that helps prevent *repressive coping,* which is dismissing or ignoring our feelings—this is bad for our health and leads to less resilient immune systems, cardiovascular disease and hypertension, and various mental health disorders (*Harvard Health Blog). I am a smart one too! If you are living here on this earth and surviving, then you are NOT a weak one either! To bear your burdens, God determined from the foundations of the world that you are strong enough to handle them all. So, as hard, or impossible as it might seem right now, YOU GOT THIS!

I am not telling you my story for 'brownie points' or for you to say, "Girl, I didn't know you went through all that!" My purpose for sharing is to let you know that "God does not show favoritism" (Romans 2:11, NIV). I am an example of the power of Christ. I want you to know that whatever you might be dealing with right now, whatever the struggle—be it low self-esteem, doubt, rejection, loss of a dream, or failures—whatever it is, God can get you through it, and IT IS NOT TOO LATE!

A VOICE STOLEN

We often think our dreams will never happen because we messed up too badly or wasted too much time. I know I did. I was always considered the 'smart one' in the family. If I'm being honest, that's all I had going for me, growing up. At least, that's what I believed. Intelligence was the only way I remember being affirmed as a young child. Of course, being well-behaved and having a neat appearance were strongly valued too, but having good grades? Child, that was like pure gold! In fact, it was way better than gold. Having good grades garnered the attention I so craved. I believe every child craves attention—and they deserve it. It shows they are valued, cherished, loved, wanted, and adored. "You are the apple of your father's eye" is a very familiar saying. Well, what happens when you don't remember what your father's eyes look like because you haven't seen him for years?

I grew up without the benefit of my father's presence for much of my life. I saw him so infrequently that I did not connect with my maiden name, 'Hammonds' (my father's last name). I did not know him, so I wanted the name I most closely associated with my identity. Lee is my mother's maiden name. So, I renamed myself 'LaShaune Lee' at five years old. I wrote it on my assignments until my kindergarten teacher asked my mother to stop me. Only God knew that I would marry the love of my life, and his name would be 'Lee.' At five years old, I called myself who I would become without knowing what I was doing.

Words and actions matter. We must be more aware of that. So, my friend, what are you saying today? It can determine your tomorrow. You can either choose to remain stuck in a hole of self-doubt and feelings of low self-worth (and I still struggle with that at times) or use your challenges as fuel for the journey. Today, I can speak to you as an overcomer because I chose to turn my pain into purpose. I am sure my father did his best with what he had at the time.

I am not here to bash him in any way. God had a purpose, even in that abandonment. "When my father and mother forsake me, then the Lord will take care of me" (Psalm 27:10 NKJV). The Lord never left my side. I walk in ordered steps, and so do you!

Father is defined in the dictionary as "a male parent" or "a man in relation to his child or children." I am going deeper in my description because I believe the role of a true father is much greater than previously stated. He is a covering, a protector, and a provider. He is a champion, a warrior, and a teacher. A father is the one you go running to when you have a problem, and he is also the one you run to with good news. A true father makes you feel safe, special, and wanted. Both seen and heard. This describes many of the fatherhood characteristics I see my husband display with our sons. I didn't have that experience with my own father. Maybe you didn't either?

You see, my parents married when I was very young—I have absolutely no memory of it. They married because that's what they were supposed to do. After all, they already had two children—my sister and me. So, get married, right? I believe love was there but not enough. They divorced shortly after, and he remarried. I did not see my father for nearly three years. My mother met someone new during his absence, and he became my father figure. And life was great for a while. By the time I saw my biological father again, I had been molested by my stepfather's father at 5 years old. And nobody knew. Because, back then, children were 'seen and not heard.' It was a terrible thing—a trauma I would not wish upon anyone. It is a bell you cannot un-ring, a Pandora's box that cannot be closed once opened. It exposed me—and I am sure it exposed some of you to a world you could not handle. Why would you be equipped to deal with such trauma? I told you that the devil tried early in my life to destroy me. To kill me. Because that is what he does. But guess what? I AM STILL HERE! YOU ARE STILL HERE! "And they overcame him by the blood of the Lamb and by the word of their testimony" (Rev. 12:11 NKJV).

I wondered and worried for a long time why I was not a 'daddy's girl.' Why was I not good enough for him to stay for me or my sister? What troubles could have been avoided if he were present to tell me "You are so pretty" or "I love you" (more often because he does love me) or "You can be anything you want to be?" How many pitfalls could have been avoided if those affirmations (emotional support or encouragement) had been shared with me? Maybe you feel like that too? In searching to fill that void, I looked for meaningful substance where there was none—the world! And just like the devil, the world does what the world is supposed to do—take! For the world is carnal, and it is selfish.

I was always searching for acceptance and affirmation. As a child growing up in the 70s, those life-giving, character-building words were not regularly used. Positive parental practices were not demonstrated often enough, so parents had some education on properly raising children. There were no resources widely available back then. Who could I run to and tell "A man touched me in my private areas, and it was causing all kinds of feelings like shame, disgust, and horror to rise in me?" There was no one. I thought I would get in trouble; this had to be my fault, right? So, I said nothing and hoped that somehow, because I told my abuser to leave, and he did, the terrible thoughts would go away. But they didn't. Nah, those jokers remained. Sidebar—I am a licensed clinical social worker by trade, and I often tell my clients, "Whatever you don't deal with will deal with you until you *deal with it*!" That is a true statement, but I did not have a *me* growing up. So, of course, I made mistakes! I let people tell me who I should be. And the message I received was, "You're not good enough." What messages have you received during the course of your life? Words have power attached to them—those spoken over you and those that are not! Be very aware of what you are saying TO yourself and what you allow others to speak OVER you. "Words kill, words give life; they're either poison or fruit—you choose" (Proverbs 18:21, MSG).

Life can be dark and lonely if not for the Light of the world—Jesus! I didn't know the Light then, so I did the best I could; I survived. (Can I get an amen from somebody out there?) But God! Because of Him, nothing is ever wasted! So, the troubles you have endured are not for nothing—it is working for your good and God's glory! If you let it, if you allow yourself to grow from your pain, your Light will shine and guide someone else out of their dark places. Like I am doing for you right now. See how that works?

A VOICE FOUND

One thing about affirmations is that they are EMPOWERING! Whether spoken over you by a valued person in your life or you speak them over yourself, they bring confidence and peace that undergirds you. Especially when the weight of this world seems to never stop bearing down on your shoulders with its constant pressures to fit in. With its demands, reminders of past failures, comparisons to others' successes, etc. We can spend a lifetime in a perpetual rabbit hole chasing the acceptance that comes from people (and that can be subjective and often shady). Or we can choose to stand in the power of knowing who God says we are and who He created us to be! I wish I had known that earlier in life, if I am being honest with you. I fell hard for the 'okey-dokey,' the 'shenanigans,' and the 'foolery' (you can fill in the blank with your favorite word).

What I am trying to get you to understand is simply this: none of that matters now! Start from where you are, learn the lesson, and move on. It is entirely possible. Life is not over for you! No, sweetie, it is not too late for you! So, what if you had an abortion? I had two before turning 18. So, what if you are a single mom? I had a child at 21, had to drop out of college, lost a job, lost my apartment, and was on welfare. According to every statistic you could read in any study conducted in this country, I should not be where I am today. But here I stand. I am making a progressive, life-changing impact in the lives of young girls. I possess the passion, drive, and EMPATHY to help them—it burns inside me. Why? Because I AM THEM! I was where they are right now—sometimes lost, confused, beat down by people's opinions, looking for hope in wanting somebody to tell me that I am good enough just being myself, letting me know "I see you." God did that for me. He saw me from the beginning. It took me a long time to see myself as He does, but thanks be to Jesus, I do now (slowly but surely). Let me help you 'cause it's dangerous out here in these 'people-pleasing' streets!

Every decision you make comes from a place. It is the outcome of whatever was poured into you—or not. If your experiences have built up your confidence, allowing you to have room to explore during your development, time to rest, time to learn from mistakes (without shame) and celebrate your achievements, then, Sis, I am happy for you. I may be somewhat jealous, in fact. I don't know if it was due to my being a *girl* or a *black girl* or a *poor black girl* or a *poor black girl raised primarily by a single mother* that brought about the causes of my struggle with low self-esteem. I don't know. As I stated earlier, my parents did the best they could based on who they were, what they had, and what they knew about child-rearing in the 70s. However, it wasn't enough to keep me from longing to be liked or accepted.

I often felt like I had to be somebody other than myself to be welcomed into the fold. I was a people pleaser simply because *I wanted to belong*. It is a dangerous position to have such a powerful need to belong and not have a safe harbor. Why? Because a person will do anything to get that need met. You are often left feeling empty, even more alone (in a room full of people), and have usually made horrible mistakes like me. I was in a pit of isolation that nearly destroyed me. Because I listened to my flesh with its constant demands to be satisfied instead of listening to God.

I had this friend I was close to—way too close to. It did not begin that way, but as time passed, my boundaries became nearly non-existent as this friendship became closer than my marital bond. It was closer than my bond with God. I saw the disaster signs— screaming at me to STOP, but I figured I must be tripping. Maybe even making up what was clearly ringing in my spirit. I chose not to listen to the Holy Spirit because I was too busy listening to my flesh, and the friendship felt good TO me, even though ultimately it was not good FOR me. You can find a way to justify anything you want to 'make it make sense.' And I did that. I made this friendship very meaningful to me—I depended on it. My day did not go right if I did not talk to my best friend. My attitude would shift. I would not feel fulfilled. Crazy, right? I made sure to take care of my family's needs, but I would ensure I had my 'me time' to spend with my best friend. We talked on the phone for hours. We hung out all the time. I figured it must be all right because my husband knew him, and they were cool. I was not only dancing close to the line of having an emotional affair; I believe I was right on that line—over that line. How offensive to God and my family!

But before you judge me (and I sincerely hope you don't), understand something I have realized—it really did start in my childhood! I do not offer that as an excuse for my actions. Still, to reiterate, this friendship conundrum directly resulted from the emotional shape I was in, having survived my traumas—not fully dealt with at that point. Molestation opened my eyes to sexual things. I was in no way mentally or emotionally ready for that at five years old. But it happened, and that exposure negatively shaped my development. As things happen in the natural realm, they also happen in the spiritual realm. I believe when I was molested, there was a spirit of shame attached to me, a spirit of lust, and a spirit of fear. So, the idea of making a new friend was out of the question because I was afraid of being alone! The attraction to him eventually was sexual in thought because the lustful spirit was still attached to me. Then the boundaries became very broad. I was losing myself. I hear you saying, "But, wait a minute; didn't you have a family, a church family, and other friends?" Yes, I did. And I still screwed up.

I should have ended the friendship when God told me to. I should not have gotten so close to him. I should never have let him replace God in my life. I just wanted a friend. I tried to fill that void that was still in me. Being married to a wonderful man didn't fill it. Having beautiful children didn't fill it. That craving for acceptance was still there because I did not deal with it. To be clear, I never had a physical affair; this is not that kind of story. But if not for God, it could have gone another way. God blocked it—*I was not that strong.*

What did this friendship fulfill, really? It filled that void I mentioned—temporarily and at a high cost. I had never really got to the root of my issues up to that point. And let me just say that if you do not get to the heart of any situation, I don't care what it is; it always comes back. I did not get to the root cause of my void then. I am learning today that I need help with that. I am learning that it is okay to ask for help. I have always been the person that could be relied on to help others and not make them feel shame about it, so why not me? I feel like I am not alone here; how about you? But I get it. I understand. When you struggle with disappointment and mistrust for so long, you learn to depend on M-E, not G-O-D. That was my mistake. Maybe you can relate to this.

Early in life, I was given a set of challenges to face (including child abuse, sexual abuse, and poverty, just to name a few) without the right resources to help me navigate those minefields. I am the oldest child on both sides of my family. I often say that the oldest child is the 'experiment.' What I mean by that is, you don't know what kind of parent you will be until you are one! I do not care what people may offer as their own experiences. All of that is wonderful, but parenthood is an experience you do not fully appreciate until it is your turn. Again, my parents did their best and are genuinely wonderful people I deeply respect and love. But they were flawed in my upbringing, as I am flawed in my children's upbringing. Let me set you free. NOBODY is perfect in this! So, a void was created, and it influenced every decision I made—before Jesus and after Jesus. Let me say something else mind-blowing to you: choosing to follow Christ does not absolve you from your life's unresolved traumas and troubles! No, baby; they intensify! God has to heal and change us, and it is PAINFUL! That is why Jesus blessed us with therapists!

Last sidebar—those who know me know how much I love my sons. I am very close to my family. I love my husband with all that is within me, and I love my sons! That motherhood bond cannot be explained; it must be experienced. My sons have my entire heart. Despite aborting my first two pregnancies, they are God's gift to me. God allowed me to be a mother. Each son draws me closer to God in different ways. My oldest son shows me God's grace and mercy as an unwed mother. My youngest son shows me God's promise. My bonus son shows me God's favor. If you want to see me fight, mess with one of mine! I told you I wasn't always saved, right? Any tough decision or immovable obstacle is nothing to me if it jeopardizes the well-being of my children or if I have to choose between anyone and my children. Even a people pleaser like me.

There came a time when I had to 'pay the piper,' as they say. It was either letting go of this friendship as God instructed me to do or losing my oldest son's respect and ruining our relationship. I chose to let go of the friendship. It came at a terrible emotional cost to me. And it took me years of isolation to fully understand why everything happened the way it did. But I did learn. I learned to never give a person that much power over me (and this is not to blame the person—I freely gave my power away)! I gave my power away to belong. Maybe you have faced a similar situation. It might not have been a person as it was in my case. Perhaps it is your job, your ministry, or your desperate need to portray yourself or your life as something it is not. All of it to make people believe in you. All to make people accept you and want to be around you. All to make people like you. Please, let me admonish you; STOP IT! Anything or anyone that you put in front of God or hold in higher esteem than God is going to get you into BIG TROUBLE. Point blank, period!

All of the things I wanted to receive from people, God already had for me! **I rejected HIM**! *And I was already saved*! There, I said it—it's out there. The King of kings and the Lord of lords wanted me, and I COULD NOT SEE IT! I lowered my standards and put all of my attention on people! How could I? Very simple—I did not think I was good enough from the root, and the devil knew it! As usual, the trap(s) were set. And even though I was warned of a major pitfall (God with His amazing grace that I don't deserve), I fell into the trap … hard. It should have killed me, and it nearly did. But God! No matter how stupid I was. "No weapon that is formed against you shall prosper" (Isaiah 54:17 NKJV). Not even the weapon of low self-esteem. Why was the devil after my self-esteem? Because he knows the power inside of me—and you! And he is scared! So he tried early in my life to steal my voice. What he actually did (with his dumb self) was to PUSH MY VOICE OUT! Every hardship I ever endured was to develop, strengthen, and get me to a place where I could be used by God to help deliver you! What a wonderful feeling to KNOW God is in control over our lives! There has never been a time when He was not. "All things work together for our good" (See Romans 8:28) and God's glory. So, let's go!

Why am I sharing all of this with you, my friend? Because I don't want you to give up on YOU! Yes, life is tough sometimes. It can be unfair. But it is not too late for any of us to turn our lives around. Give it to God. Allow Him to 'reset' your thinking and give you a new perspective. All is not lost, and it is not over—YOU ARE STILL HERE! AND YOU ARE WORTH IT TO GOD! He loves you and wants to help. Let Him! Take your hands off the steering wheel and let God drive. He knows what is best FOR you, and only God can get the best out of you! Give your life to Him and watch what happens! I am a living, breathing witness to God's ability to do the impossible. I should not be here. I should not be in my right mind. I should not be even used by the Almighty, but here I am!

The devil could not destroy me, and he cannot destroy you either. We have a say in the matter and a God who has our back. We cannot be stopped! Who would have thought a child raised under my circumstances would ever amount to anything? God did. Things happened to me, as they surely have happened to you to throw you off your pre-destined journey. Or did they? I don't think so. Remember, ALL things are working for our good, right? The devil did try, and still does, but he is a defeated foe.

When I was molested, I stood up to my abuser, and not only did he stop, but he also fled! I used my voice! That experience causes me to fight for others like I am fighting for you! I was overpowered by an adult who should have known better. But I made my voice heard. You can use your voice too! I have been bullied and briefly was a bully. (I'm sure you didn't see that one coming, did you?). But I refused to stay there. I refused to let adverse life events become an excuse for why I did not become all that God designed for me to become. Don't let that happen to you!

You can get up and have a new outcome. Right now. Through tears and breakdowns. Through trials and tribulations. The ups and downs of it all. You can make it! God will help you. He will send you help. You can have Jesus and a therapist! Clinical social workers make great therapists (I should know). Who are those supportive friends and family members who want to see you win? Connect with them; there is safety in numbers. Do not self-isolate. Look for resources in your local area and make a call. Help is out there. Do not be afraid. Here are some resources to get you started:

- **Call or text 988** if you are feeling suicidal or in a mental crisis.
- **988lifeline.org** – lists practical steps for getting help and organizations to meet your mental health needs, with a special emphasis on the mental health needs of the black community.
- **nimh.nih.gov** - lists practical steps for getting help and organizations to meet your mental health needs, including ̄eterans. (Thank you for your sacrifice!)
  - i.org – offers local support, mental health education, and ɔacy.
    - a.gov - lists practical steps for getting help and ations to meet your mental health and substance abuse

God is waiting for your yes. Say yes to Him today. Let God heal you. Let Him choose your friends. Let Him give you "beauty for ashes" (Isaiah 61:3 NKJV). Somebody is waiting for you to answer your call. YOU are the answer to a prayer. YOU are the example in your family of a gracious and merciful God. Don't allow the devil to mute your testimony. SHUT HIS MOUTH! You have the power through Jesus Christ to do just that. And if, by chance, you don't know Jesus Christ in the pardon of your sins, YOU TOTALLY CAN! Give your life to Him today, right now, right from where you are. Romans 10:9 says, "If you declare with your mouth, 'Jesus is Lord,' and believe in your heart that God raised Him from the dead, you will be saved." (NIV)

God is the only reason I am alive today. God is the only reason I am done with trying to please people. God is the only one that can fill any void I feel. God raised me from nothing. God chose me, even though I sometimes think I have nothing important to give. God used my story to deliver you, to set you free. I am because God is! And s are you! Be free in Jesus' name! Freedom is a choice. Choose wise and watch God work! God loves you, and so do I. Let's get it don

Defying the Odds
Katrina V. Perry

I was raised in a loving home. I was 'Mommy's baby' and 'Daddy's little girl.' The youngest of six, I was spoiled but well-rounded. I loved to read, write, sing, and play outdoors. I maintained good grades in school and made the honor roll. I was even selected to be in an academically gifted and talented program. I was raised in the church. I gave my life to Christ at a young age and got baptized. As I grew older, I made unwise choices despite being a smart kid. You see, there was this boy I liked. We were junior high and high school sweethearts. He was an elder's son, and I was a deacon's daughter. We spent much time in church but craved life's excitement outside of the church. He was adventurous, whereas I was curious and captivated.

We hung out with kids who liked skipping school. Schools were not strict back then. If you showed up to homeroom, they considered you present for the day. We planned which day to skip and whose house we would party at. We checked in during homeroom, slipped out of a side door, and met up at someone's house whose parents were at work. While having fun with my friends, I somehow kept my grades up. I was active in the school chorus, a pageant, and band front. I was also involved in the church's youth choir, youth usher board, vacation Bible school, Christmas and Easter programs, and a church pageant.

My mom occasionally asked if I was 'out there messing around,' and I always denied it. I guess I was a great actress too. I was physically fit and active. I played outdoor sports with the neighborhood kids. I was excited to play junior varsity basketball. I didn't make the team because I couldn't keep up with the rest of the squad. Why? Because I was having a baby. My facade crumbled. My parents, although disappointed, were not hostile. They didn't browbeat or belittle me. Instead, they counseled me and prayed for me. They encouraged me. So, as our parents had 'the meeting,' he and I watched sheepishly as they discussed plans to move forward. I remember how full my heart was, experiencing them meeting for the first time and genuinely liking each other. We were blessed because our baby had grandparents, aunts, and uncles from both sides, who were present and available. So, at 15 years old, I gave birth to my first child. You can imagine the things people said behind my back. That I'd ruined two lives and inconvenienced everyone. But God defied the odds of their negativity because my beautiful baby was born into a village of love and support.

But life dealt a devastating blow. My mother unexpectedly passed away when my child was 3 months old. My entire world fell apart. I felt like I was in a movie theater, watching my life on the big screen. This couldn't be real! What was I going to do? I mean, I was her *baby,* and she was my *everything.* My heart was shattered into a million pieces. I found myself trying to be a mother to this sweet and helpless child while feeling like a helpless child myself. Not knowing how to deal with my grief, I coped by hanging out and doing what 'teens gone wild' do. We continued to skip school and drink alcohol at house parties. God's grace, mercy, and my village sustained me because I stayed in school and maintained good grades. I attended church occasionally but didn't put much effort into connecting with God. I can't describe how I felt then, but my grief prevented me from drawing close.

I took the path of least resistance by relying on my child's father for emotional support and continued having unprotected sex with him. I found out I was pregnant again, and we gave birth to our second child when I was 17. Although an emotional wreck, I held my head as high as possible and embraced my beautiful new baby. My dad and his parents admonished us but continued to lovingly support us. I thank God I didn't have to endure negativity from our families. Their grace and kindness kept me from going off the deep end. But this time, I didn't have to worry about what people said behind my back because some said how they felt right to my face. "So, what are you going to do with yourself now?" "How are you going to raise two kids?" "Girl, you couldn't wait to graduate before having another one?"

As a teenager, it was difficult to emotionally process these comments, so I turned to food for solace. And I stayed in 'teen gone wild' mode. In my mind, life was spiraling out of control. I couldn't wrap my head around what was going on. It was one thing after another. But I had a family that prayed for me. And I know now that God kept His hand on me. After my first baby was born, my mom shared with me how she and her friend fasted and prayed for me. I faced several complications with the pregnancy and baby because of risk factors that I wasn't aware of. That was my first experience learning how the power of prayer can overcome the odds.

Naysayers didn't expect me to finish high school. But they didn't factor in God's divine purpose for my life. Their analysis was flawed because they made calculations based on human understanding of the facts presented. Jeremiah 29:11 (NIV) reads, "'For I know the plans I have for you,' declares the Lord, 'plans to prosper you and not to harm you, plans to give you hope and a future.'" I came to my senses and decided to attend summer school and take classes ahead of schedule. God defied the odds, and I graduated a year early in summer school. Although I wasn't where I needed to be in my relationship with God, I acknowledged my dependence on Him and that He would help me get to where I needed to be. I refused to accept what society said might become of me and my children.

So now what? I knew I wanted to be a productive member of society, so I got a job. I wanted my children to grow up in the same home as their father, so we got married. I obtained a certificate in Electronics Technology from a technical college. Sadly, our marriage and finances were in trouble after only a few years. Again, I coped by partying and eating. Neither one filled the voids. I gained more weight while feeling depressed and empty inside. But God showed grace, mercy, and favor. I was offered a life-changing career opportunity. I still remember my father-in-law's prophetic words when I told him the good news, "God gave you that job for a reason." So, although my marriage ended, my children were provided for. And I would be remiss not to mention that my village stayed right by my side. Their love and support to help me raise my children was paramount.

And yet life still wasn't done throwing curveballs. Eleven years after losing my mom, my dad passed away. I was his 'stinker,' and he was my hero. My loving and gentle giant. While I thought I was in a better space emotionally to deal with losing him because it wasn't sudden, I still made bad decisions and used food to cope. Over the next few years, I became dangerously overweight.

I contended with even more emotional baggage as I experienced disappointments in my professional career. I realized my position had no promotion potential, so I obtained my Associate of Science degree in Social Sciences. I began undergraduate courses but took a break. I have plans to complete the requirements to receive my Bachelor of Interdisciplinary Studies degree. The enemy tricked me into thinking that I would never advance. I was repeatedly passed over for laterals and promotions. The biggest disappointment was not being selected for a position I spent years preparing for, was well qualified for, and assumed I would get. My coworkers and some of the managers agreed I was a shoo-in.

I felt the odds were in my favor because I had begun rebuilding my relationship with God. I figured God had my back on this one. But God said, "No." Devastated doesn't begin to describe how I felt. Embarrassed is an understatement. But I believe that God had to humble me. I was too sure of myself. I wasn't spiritually prepared for a promotion. So, I decided that even if I was never promoted, I would always give one hundred percent. Everything I did at work was going to be for God's glory. When I stopped trying to impress people, it turned out they were impressed! I remembered a prophecy from a family member who said I would retire well above the position I aspired to. Proverbs 16:3 (NIV) reads, "Commit to the Lord whatever you do, and He will establish your plans." It was during a general conversation, but now I heed when someone speaks into my life. 1 Corinthians 2:9 (NKJV) reads, "But as it is written: 'Eye has not seen, nor ear heard, nor have entered into the heart of man the things which God has prepared for those who love Him.'" And God blew my mind! My latest promotion far exceeded what I prayed for. God's denial of my prayer was just a delay for what He had planned for me. It was an unexpected and humbling experience of God's favor. Once again, God defied the odds that I wouldn't obtain a higher education or get promoted.

I share some of my life's stories to encourage others. No matter what has happened or what you've done, God has a purpose and a plan for your life. God said in Jeremiah 1:5a (NIV), "Before I formed you in the womb I knew you, before you were born I set you apart." We are all special and precious to God. Don't let your circumstances separate you from God. The odds may not appear to be in your favor. But God will defy the odds so that He gets the glory. I'm finding my voice as I continue to grow in the Lord. I'm walking in boldness and embracing what has happened in my life so that I can help someone else. I am learning to lean on God during trials instead of turning to destructive devices and behaviors. I refuse to let the enemy trick me into thinking that my past experiences will define my future.

Those experiences taught me valuable lessons about how the enemy tried to kill and silence me. I was in situations I shouldn't have survived. I let my health get out of control. I listened to naysayers who wanted to crush my spirit. But I am who God says I am! I am an overcomer! "I will not die; instead, I will live to tell what the LORD has done" (Psalm 118:17, NLT). I learned that accepting Jesus as my Lord and Savior and letting God take control will turn the odds in my favor. I didn't always get it right, but God's grace and mercy kept me and my family.

The Bible guarantees that I'll never face trials and tribulations alone if I keep my hands in God's hands. Deuteronomy 31:6 says, "Be strong and courageous. Do not be afraid or terrified because of them, for the Lord your God goes with you; He will never leave you nor forsake you." (NIV) I had so many reasons to give up. I often think about the roads I could have taken and the choices I could have made. To be honest, I'm not proud of some of the adult decisions I made. I could have and probably should have lost my mind. Grief, ignorance, and living in survival mode fueled a lot of my bad decisions. But God forgives. I was never so deep in sin that God couldn't reach me. Once I understood that we all can come back to God, and His grace is sufficient, I began to let Him take control so that I could take control.

God defied the odds regarding my personal life by blessing me with family, friends, and mentors who supported all areas of my life. Proverbs 27:9 (TPT) says, "Sweet friendships refresh the soul and awaken our hearts with joy, for good friends are like the anointing oil that yields the fragrant incense of God's presence." My spiritual, emotional, and physical well-being have all improved because I aligned myself with the right tribe. I have friends who pray for and with me. I have friends who counsel me. I have friends who are my oasis. Some encouraged me by exercising with me. We walked and talked about how God has sustained us through our fiery trials. As I released over 75 pounds of physical weight, I also released the spiritual weight of my past. But the most cherished friendships I have are with my children. What society probably considered my downfall turned out to be my greatest achievement. My children are my best friends and inspiration. Because of them, I look forward to holidays instead of being depressed. We have a special bond because it was us against the world at one time. When I wanted to give up, those sweet faces, eyes, smiles, and unconditional love they had for the teenager they called 'Ma' kept me going. That foundation makes the bond with my grandchildren even more special.

I recall a day when my mom and I were in the kitchen. She was sweeping the floor and saying her fervent prayer was that all her children would be saved. And as a mother and grandmother, I completely understand now. I don't know what she envisioned for her baby girl's future, but I know she had faith in God. Luke 1:45 (NIV) reads, "Blessed is she who has believed that the Lord would fulfill his promises to her!" What were the odds that a teenage mother of two by age 17 would graduate from high school a year early, obtain higher education, excel in her career, and become a published author? And that's just the beginning. I am resting in the favor of God's promises. Man's analysis of my situation would probably say the odds were stacked against me. However, the odds are defied when God is in control and His hand is on you.

Conclusion

Wow! Take a deep breath with me. What an awesome display of God's love, faithfulness, grace, and His unwavering presence in our lives. I know you, like me, have been blessed by reading the powerful stories in this book.

It is my sincere desire that the stories in this book have touched your heart, enhanced your faith, stirred your heart, and more importantly, helped you to see God in a new way, a more pronounced way, and greatly affirmed your love for Him.

I encourage you to reach out personally to the co-author or co-authors whose stories impacted you. I also want to encourage you to consider sharing your story. We all have a story! Just like the stories in this book that have touched you, someone needs to read your story too.

If you are interested in participating in one of my book projects, please email me directly at **manifestblessings@yahoo.com**.

Thank you so much for taking this Faith Journey with us. I pray God's richest blessings on you!

Spreading Faith One Book & One Story At A Time!
Dr. Nicole S. Mason, Esq.

Meet the Co-Authors

Priscilla Ademola

Priscilla is a wife, mother, gifted dancer, and anointed psalmist. She walks in a powerful prophetic gift and serves alongside her husband in ministry in Armhem, Netherlands. Priscilla serves as a pastoral counselor using her powerful story of victory to help women change their lives by seeing themselves as God sees them and not through the lens of trauma and tragedy.

A beautiful soul and a mighty force to be reckoned with describe Priscilla. She is indeed a warrior in the Kingdom of God! God is using her to bring healing and freedom to women globally! Her story is going to bless you tremendously!
FB – Priscilla Hoogwood Ademola

Trashawna Carter

Trashawna R. Carter is a wife, mother, entrepreneur, and servant leader, but most importantly, Trashawna is a SURVIVOR, who NOW understands the saying that "God will not put more on you than you can bear." There is nothing like being told you are nothing. Life has taught Shawna many lessons, but the greatest lesson that she has learned is that her strength comes from within and that she can do all things through Christ (Philippians 4:13).

She went from having pain growing up to living a purposeful adult life. It is her faith that has brought her this far. And she has put in the work. Childhood trauma can be devastating if not dealt with. She knows all too well that trauma cannot be 'swept under the rug' but MUST be dealt with. And forgiveness and healing must follow. Her life's mantra is, "Never look down on anyone because it could be you."
FB – Shawna R. Carter
IG – Trashawna Carter

Michelle Clark

Michelle Clark is a mother, grandmother, minister, and make-up artist. Michelle loves to combine her ministry with her love for beauty and fashion. She has been in the beauty industry for 10 years.

Her love for make-up artistry has afforded her opportunities to work for Macy's as a beauty consultant for Lancome, Elizabeth Arden, Fashion Fair, and Christian Dior.

Michelle has also served as a make-up artist for a number of fashion shows and beauty pageants. Additionally, her work has also been showcased in magazines.
FB – Michelle A. Clark

Dr. Aikyna Finch

Dr. Aikyna Finch is a podcaster, social media coach, and TEDx speaker. She coaches in Empowerment, Life, and Social Media at the individual and group levels from her company, Finch and Associates, LLC. She is the host of the Dr. Finch Experience® Podcast broadcasted by her company, Changing Minds Online™. She speaks and livestreams on Motivation, Education, and Social Media. In 2018, she founded the Social Power Summit, an event with a Live and Virtual component for Women in STEM and People of Color in Social Media to have a platform where they can shine. In 2020, she started her tech coaching brand called Technically Intuitive®. It began as a column she wrote on The Coach Guardian, and from there, this brand now includes training on social media and technology. In November 2022, she became a TEDX DeerPark Speaker with her presentation on "The Benefits of AI on Social Media." Currently, she is a member of the DEIB Training and Development Subcommittee of the International Coaching Federation, where she is a DEIB facilitator. She spoke at the ICF Converge Conference in August 2023. She is a Board member for ICF Tennessee and three other organizations.

Dr. Finch is the co-author of twelve books. She launched her first solo project, Motivation Ignited, in November 2016 and compiled her first anthology project, Empowerpreneurs, in February 2020. She is a contributor to Huffington Post, Goalcast, Forbes, and Thrive Global. She has been interviewed and featured on the Huffington Post, Hello Beautiful, Women Speakers Association, International Coach Federation, and many others. She has spoken on many platforms, including ICF Tennessee Chapter, Periscope Summit, Women In Leadership Summit, The Success Women Summit, The Business Vlog Summit, and many more! She can be found at @DrADFinch on all Social Media Platforms.

Dr. Finch is an educator. She received a Doctorate of Management, an MBA in Technology Management, and an Executive MBA from Colorado Technical University. She has an MS in Management in Marketing, an MS in Information Systems in IT Project Management from Strayer University, and a BS in Aeronautical Technology in Industrial Electronics from the School of Engineering of Tennessee State University. She is a former Campus and Faculty Dean who established three campuses' enrollment records. She was also a Faculty and Coach Trainer and helped several faculty and staff members become coaches. Her teaching disciplines include business, leadership, marketing, social media, and information systems at the graduate and undergraduate levels. She has published over 30 academic publications and presented on youth and adult education, social media, and job search topics.

www.aikynafinch.com
FB – DrAikyna Finch
IG – DrADFinch

Minister Da'Mali Goings

Minister Goings (MG) is an inventive humble servant whose life emulates a true giving spirit evangelizing a resounding message of hope and recognizing self-worth while living a life of love intentionally on purpose. A mother of three, grandmother of four, and spiritual mother to many, certified lay minister, health minister, Christian life coach, international speaker, and author, Da'Mali is known for her love, dedication, and commitment to those she serves.

With over 20 years in ministry as a spiritual visionary & midwife, teacher, and intercessor, she incorporates her love and care for people through the instructions from the voice of God while bringing a prophetic message that resonates in the hearts of those she connects with, leaving the imprint of God's love on their hearts.

She received her call to ministry as a child but fully embraced ministry and the call to teach, preach, and evangelize through baptism at the age of 30. From this time, she has been on the path to help restore as many people to Christ as she possibly can through her service, witness, and testimony.

Having received education and training beginning in 2009, she became certified as a CLM (Certified Lay Minister) in the United Methodist Church and in 2017 received certification in Health Ministry through Wesley Theological School, certification as a Mental Health First Aider for Youth and Adults and attended Lancaster Bible College with a focus in Biblical Studies. In addition, she has over 24 years of experience in the customer service field which has led her to a purposeful marketplace coaching and consulting business (Middle Marketplace Cultivators). She is a licensed massage therapist and uses her knowledge from this field to introduce healing throughout her ministry.

She has served in many capacities within the church such as Youth Leader, Single Women's Ministry Coordinator, Children and Adult Sunday School Teacher, and Bible Study Facilitator and currently serves on the Ministerial Team at Grace UMC, Fort Washington, where she is the Convener of the Worship Ministry. She also serves on the Abundant Health Ministry & Young People's Ministry for the Baltimore Washington Conference and is the Washington East District's Youth Coordinator.

She loves studying, meditating, and praying the Word of God. One of her favorite scriptures is Romans 8:18 (AMP), "For I consider [from the standpoint of faith] that the sufferings of the present life are not worthy to be compared with the glory that is about to be revealed to us *and* in us," and her favorite quote is by Dr. Maya Angelou, "Life is not measured by the breaths we take but by the moments that take our breath away." No matter the accomplishments or titles, she just wants to be recognized as a child and servant of God as she works in the vineyard, gleaning souls for Christ!
www.ministerd.com
FB – Minister Goings
IG – DaMali Goings

Elaine Harris

Elaine Harper Harris invites you on a transformative journey through her inspiring biography. With a focus on faith, empowerment, and resilience, Elaine's story captivates readers, leaving an indelible mark on their hearts and minds.

Born and raised in Pittsburgh, Pennsylvania, Elaine's journey is rooted in her unwavering faith in God and her deep commitment to making a difference in the lives of others. She carries the legacy of her late parents, Ralph G. Harper and Marion Jane Graves Harper, who instilled in her the values of compassion, integrity, and service.

Education became a cornerstone of Elaine's quest to uplift the vulnerable and oppressed. After graduating from Saint Cecilia's Academy in Washington, D.C., Elaine pursued her passion for social welfare, earning a bachelor's degree in Sociology with a concentration in Social Welfare from Virginia State University in 1981. Her thirst for knowledge continued to grow, and in 2020, she proudly received her Master of Social Work from Walden University. Elaine's unwavering commitment to excellence is further reflected in her pursuit of a Doctorate in social work from Walden University, where she seeks to expand her impact and deepen her understanding of societal issues.

Elaine's professional journey has been defined by her relentless dedication to advocacy and social change. Working with older adults, she has spent 38 years as the Director of Social Services for skilled nursing and rehabilitation facilities across the Washington, D.C., Metropolitan area. Through her work, she has been a beacon of hope for countless individuals, ensuring they receive the care and support they deserve.

An active member of Greater Mt Calvary Holy Church in Washington, D.C., for the past 40 years, Elaine's commitment to her faith community has been unwavering. She has held esteemed positions such as the founder and past president of the homeless ministry, a member of the associate missionary board, and a vital member of the Women of Virtue. Elaine served as the past Secretary of Alfred A. Owen's family life center, leaving an indelible mark on the community.

Elaine's devotion to her church and her faith have not gone unnoticed. In 1996, they honored her with the Woman of the Year award, recognizing her extraordinary contributions to her community. Her unshakeable belief in the power of faith, as inspired by Hebrews 11:1, has guided her through life's challenges and triumphs, allowing her to affect the lives of those around her in immeasurable ways.

Central to Elaine's journey is her experience as a devoted mother to her beloved son, Devin. Born with developmental delays, Devin's presence has shaped Elaine's perspective on life, motherhood, and the strength found in unwavering love. Through her upcoming book, Elaine shares her deeply personal experiences, offering a beacon of hope to other parents navigating similar paths. Her story sheds light on the joys, struggles, and triumphs encountered along the way, serving as a source of inspiration and support for families facing similar challenges.

Beyond her role as a mother, Elaine extends her compassion and expertise to support families in need of long-term care for their loved ones. As a trusted consultant, she helps navigate the complexities of Medicaid and Medicare, ensuring families make informed decisions and find suitable facilities that meet their unique needs. Elaine's advocacy extends to families of children and adults with disabilities, tirelessly working to bridge disparities and empower individuals to reach their full potential.

In addition to her consultancy work, Elaine collaborates with local non-profit community service organizations such as Sarah's Hands, Strategic Music Partnership, and the True Vines Center. Alongside her loving husband, Henry, Elaine is instrumental in planning events like Senior Night Out, a cherished evening of Christian music and the Arts that brings joy and connection to older adults in nursing facilities and the wider community.

Married for 38 years, Elaine's love story with her husband, Henry W. Harris, Sr., is a testament to their unwavering commitment to one another. Together, they have nurtured a beautiful family, raising four children: Henry, Jr.; Jason; Devin; and Brittany. Elaine finds immense joy in the addition of her daughter-in-law, Dina, and the love she shares with her three granddaughters, Deja, Lala, and Khloe'. Family has been the foundation of Elaine's strength, supporting her through life's challenges and inspiring her to persevere.

Elaine Harper Harris's biography serves as a powerful testament to her extraordinary character, unwavering dedication, and profound faith. Through her story, she illuminates the power of faith, resilience, and compassion, leaving an indelible impact on her readers. As she embraces her calling to uplift and empower others, Elaine's biography resonates deeply with family, friends, members of her church community, and readers seeking solace, inspiration, and guidance in their own spiritual journeys.

www.elaineharperharris.com
FB – Elaine Harris
IG – Elaine Harris737

Deborah Johnson

Deborah M. Johnson is the daughter of Bishop Weldon M. Johnson and the late Jacqueline Robinson Johnson. She is the mother of two beautiful children, Brooke Elena and Jayden Eric Johnson. A 1998 graduate from the University of Maryland Eastern Shore, she also studied at Iowa State University and completed the Women's Entrepreneurship Certificate Program at Cornell University. She holds a master's certificate in Government Contracting from George Washington University and has worked in the federal government with the Department of Justice for 15 years as a Contracting Officer.

Deborah is the founder and CEO of Visions D'Vine LLC. As a Master Makeup Artist, she has used this business to combine her passion with her purpose to transform clients from the inside out. A graduate from Von Lee International School of Aesthetics in Pikesville, MD, under the Makeup Artistry Program, Deborah received her Maryland State License in Makeup Artistry in 2008. She further studied and also became certified in Eyebrow Threading. She advanced her skills by attending various seminars and symposiums, including but not limited to Sam Fine, Celebrity Makeup Artist—Fine Beauty Tour; MAC Pro Classes; Mini Bridal Workshop taught by Celebrity Makeup Artist Candace Corey; Eye Makeup Class sponsored by Last Looks Makeup Academy taught by Jennifer Lombardo; and a Just Eyes Workshop led by Grammy Award winning Makeup Artist Thom Supernaut.

Her work has graced the pages of Black Sophisticate's Hair Magazine and Essere Magazine. She has provided makeup services for guest speakers on Success Filled Living Television Network and had the privilege of working with John Jessup of the Christian Broadcast Network. She has worked as a Freelance Makeup Artist for Yves Saint Laurent and Gorgio Armani. Deborah had the opportunity to work with the Glam Squad for the 2013 BET Honors under the mentorship of Celebrity Makeup Artist Kym Lee. More recently, she was the product manager for Wink and Pout by Kym Lee from 2015 to 2018. In 2017, she was the assistant makeup artist in a Juwan Lee Film entitled "Secrets" and in 2021 Deborah served as the lead makeup artist in "The Exit Row," a thriller movie written and produced by Cine30 Media.

After the passing of her mother on December 16, 2020, from a long battle with cancer, Deborah has refocused on her healing while partnering with a few photographers to begin a Survivor Series Campaign, a campaign to honor a survivor who has made it through a physical and/or emotional situation. Deborah's goal is to offer services on a monthly basis that will allow the survivor to feel special for a day by providing them with a photo shoot and mini makeover. Her mother always wanted to look her best, no matter what she might have been going through, and Deborah hopes to provide that experience to those she encounters.

Deborah is a faithful member of New Life Christian Church and Ministries in Cambridge, Maryland, under the leadership of Bishop Weldon M. Johnson. She has served on various auxiliaries within the ministry. She loves traveling, being near the water, enhancing the beauty of her clients through makeup artistry, enjoys spending time with family and pampering herself. She's a proud member of Delta Sigma Theta Sorority, Inc. Her mantra is: if she can help somebody, then her living will not be in vain.
www.visionsdvine.com
FB – Visionsdvine
IG – Visionsdvine

LaShaune Lee

LaShaune Lee is an advocate—always on the side of those who have felt unseen and unheard. She is a licensed clinical social worker. She is here to erase the stigma that remains in the black community as it relates to mental health. She is a wife and has been married for 25 years, a mother of three adult sons, and a servant of Jesus Christ by way of the GMCHC Ushers Ministry where she has served for nearly 23 years. She is called to the earth for such a time as this to deliver the brokenhearted. LaShaune Lee believes she is called for everyone and is willing to elevate people.

B.S. Family Science- UMD College Park
MSW - Howard University
Social Worker for 11 years
Director of Clinical Services for an all-girl program in Ward 8 DC that impacts the lives of girls from elementary school to young adulthood.
www.ll-elevation.com
FB – LaShaune.Lee
IG – LeeLaShaune

Chaplain Paulette McPherson

Paulette McPherson is committed to providing emotional and spiritual support for individuals of all faiths or no specific faith tradition, specializing in understanding the needs and struggles of individuals facing complex physical, spiritual, and emotional conflicts.

As a board-certified chaplain and certified professional life coach, she offers an unconventional approach to counseling, assisting individuals in setting achievable goals toward finding hope, healing, and transformation amidst adversity. Her deep passion lies in guiding others toward emotional, spiritual, and physical recovery, employing a distinctive blend of compassion, humor, and wisdom to support clients on their journey of self-discovery and personal development.

At the core of Chaplain Paulette's practice is her education. She graduated from Lancaster Bible College, summa cum laude, with a B.S. in Biblical Studies. She also has a Master of Arts degree and an M.Div. in Christian Care from Capital Seminary & Graduate School, where she graduated with honors. In addition, she has a Business Management Degree and is a doctoral candidate in a Strategic Leadership program.

Paulette operates with a unique set of skills and experiences. Previously, she was the British International School of Washington Business Administration Manager, a Broadcast Assistant for B.B.C. News (United Kingdom), and a National Health Service (United Kingdom) administrator. She has over 30 years of experience in business management and administration and more than 35 years in ministry.

Chaplain Paulette is originally from Sheffield, England, and has two adult children. She loves traveling extensively, cooking, and listening to live music in her spare time. Chaplain Paulette also has a passion for electronics, graphics, and musical instruments. She believes that if she weren't a hospital chaplain, she would probably travel the world as a bass player, drummer, or camera operator/editor for an international news bureau!
FB – Paulette McPherson

Tracy Morgan

Tracy Morgan is nationally syndicated on the Rejoice Musical Soul Food Radio Network. She is also the host of Morning Inspirations on 96.3 WHUR FM in Washington, D.C., and the Program Director and Morning Show Host on 1480 AM WBBP in Memphis, TN.

Tracy has been in the Broadcasting Communication Industry for over 30 years. For nearly a decade, she was a popular host on the CBS-owned Heaven 1580 in Washington, D.C. She has won multiple Stellar Awards, including one for Announcer of the Year. Tracy served on the Stellar Awards Gospel Music Academy Advisory Board from 2004–2010.

Tracy was awarded the Reach Award for Outstanding Achievement by an Announcer at the 2014 Stellar Awards. The Reach Awards recognizes the accolades and achievements of radio announcers. Since becoming the Program Director at 1480 WBBP in 2012, the station has been nominated for a Stellar Award six times for Large Market Radio Station of the Year. In 2015, WBBP won Radio Station of the Year Large Market under Tracy's leadership. In 2022, Tracy was the first female to be inducted into the Spin Awards Hall of Fame.

Tracy has held many positions in radio, including Program Director, Music Director, and Producer. She's worked for CBS Radio, Salem Communications, and Radio One. Tracy has maintained high ratings and popularity while hosting Mornings, Middays, and Afternoon Drive positions on the air. In 2002, Tracy started "The Tracy Morgan Radio Show" to expand her talents outside of the Washington, D.C., area. Tracy has also made several TV appearances, including The Word Network BET, and Howard University's WHUT TV 32. She's hosted her own television show "In Praise," a video gospel music program.

In 2005, Tracy was inducted into the Broadcasters Hall of Fame in Akron, Ohio. In 2014, she was inducted into the Columbia School of Broadcasting Hall of Fame where she attended. Tracy earned a Certificate in Music Industry Essentials at New York University from The Clive Davis Institute of Recorded Music under the Tisch School of the Arts.

In addition to Tracy's busy schedule in radio and television, she remains actively involved in the community. She gives back to the community with her annual "Back to School with New Shoes" campaign that helps families in need by providing new shoes for kids. Tracy's number one priority is God and her family. One of her favorite scriptures is Philippians 4:13, "I can do all things through Christ which strengtheneth me." She is married to Keith and, together, they have one daughter, Katrina.

FB – Tracy Morgan

FB – Tracy M On Air

Katrina V. Perry

A doting mother of two and grandmother of six, Katrina resides in the Hampton Roads area of Virginia. Her federal service career spans over 33 years, and she is employed in Information Technology as a Data Services Division Head. Katrina serves as Executive Director of the Praying Sisters – War Room Non-Profit Organization 501(c)(3). Their mission is to carry out The Great Commission by providing resources and programs for women. Katrina is embracing her spiritual gift of mercy-showing as a certified Death Doula. She is excited to pursue her evangelistic and shepherding spiritual gifts through various artistic outlets and mentorship projects.
www.katrinavperry.com
FB – Katrina Cary Perry

Rev. Mary L. Wilson

Reverend Mary Lewis Wilson is a native of Buffalo, New York, born to a family of preachers and spiritual leaders. Reverend Mary L. Wilson is an alumnus of Howard University where she earned a Bachelor of Arts degree in sociology and psychology. She received her Master of Divinity degree at the Howard University School of Divinity. Her scholarship and her compassion combined are the substance of a dynamic ministry that is manifested in her vision and her leadership qualities. God is glorified in the work of this Woman of God because of her innate ability to empower and encourage others.

Rev. Mary served in various capacities in ministry along with her husband, Rev. Willie F. Wilson for 44 years until her retirement due to health reasons in 2016. Reverend Wilson has distinguished herself in music ministry as a singer and a choir director. She is an original member of the Richard Smallwood singers and is known nationally for her work as the founder and original director of the Union Temple Youth Choir. She directed the choir on its debut CD, "God Reigns." The Youth Choir is unparalleled throughout the country, having performed in concerts and on national media with many outstanding artists.

Although closely identified with the music ministry, Reverend Wilson is a visionary leader and a tireless advocate for women, young adults, the poor, the oppressed, and children. She has served as the Executive Director for the Harambee House for Youth for the entire 27 years of its existence. It was an Africentric residential facility for court-adjudicated juveniles ages nine to 18.

Her most recent vocation involves being a BLESSED STROKE survivor. On January 15, 2015, she suffered an intracerebral hemorrhagic stroke. Her recovery is a TRUE miracle and despite a few lingering complications, she is determined to be 'patient with the process' and advocate for and encourage other survivors. She sponsors special recognition services and events in order to encourage, pray for, and show loving concern to survivors.

This tireless and energetic queen lives a life that is pleasing to her King and to her Father in Heaven. She infuses her warm and loving spirit and amazing sense of humor into everything that she does. She is devotion, personified. Her love for her husband, her four children, six grandchildren, and her church family glorifies God.

Reverend Mary Wilson *is a sermon* for those who would not yet come into the house of the Lord to hear a sermon.
FB – Mary L. Wilson
IG – Rev Lou Lou

Indea Webb

Indea Webb ('Lady Indea') is a daughter, sister, woman of God, prayer warrior, advocate, and humanitarian. A woman of destiny with a calling to help other women turn their ashes into beauty, she is committed, as we have been commissioned to taking the gospel around the world and ministering to women who feel 'unpretty' and have been broken by gender-based violence. She seeks to bring restoration and empowerment within an atmosphere of hope and healing. Her vision is of a world in which every woman can live a life free from violence and walk in the abundance of knowing they are fearfully and wonderfully made.

A cheesecake connoisseur, Indea loves making people laugh and helping them enjoy life to its fullest. Her favorite Scripture is Psalm 34:1 which states, "I will bless the Lord at all times: his praise shall continually be in my mouth."

Indea has worked in the space of domestic violence, human trafficking, and other forms of gender-based violence. She has traveled broadly domestically and internationally and was a past participant in the Jimmy & Rosalynn Carter Work Project, a volunteer event through Habitat for Humanity where she served as a crew leader and worked alongside 2,000 international and local volunteers to build 100 homes in Patan village, Malavli town, Lonavala, Maharashtra state, western India. Her other volunteer activities have included the National Coalition Against Domestic Violence, Food & Friends, and Ronald McDonald House Charities of Greater Washington, D.C.

Indea holds a Bachelor of Arts in International Politics from The Pennsylvania State University, a Certificate of Bible Studies, and a Certificate of Ministry from Calvary Bible Institute. Additionally, Indea has certification in Working in Contemporary Nations through the Tribal Learning Community & Educational Exchange (TLCEE) program at UCLA Extention. She has an intermediate level in Italian and is a classically trained violinist.
www.ladyindea.me
FB – Indea Webb
IG – Lady Indea

About the Visionary
Dr. Nicole S. Mason, Esquire

Born with a spirit of advocacy, Nicole knew at the age of nine that she wanted to be a lawyer. Having what she felt was the 'gift of gab,' Nicole would speak up for those that either wouldn't or couldn't speak up for themselves. She has carried this same energy into her adult life. In addition to her advocacy, Nicole is a bold, courageous, and confident woman on a mission to help other women live life and achieve success on their own terms.

As an only child and working in her grandmother's dry cleaners, Nicole is an astute businesswoman. Her grandmother pushed her to go after her dream of becoming a lawyer, but when it came time for her to apply to law school, she applied nine times and was rejected nine times. Yes, you read that correctly. She was rejected nine times. She would not take no for an answer. She applied for the 10th time and was accepted. Upon entering the orientation, some of Nicole's classmates gasped for air. They were shocked and surprised to see Nicole big, round, and pregnant and starting law school! She graduated on time with her class and passed the bar exam.

Nicole is the owner of a boutique law firm specializing in estate planning. She also operates a coaching and speaking business. She intentionally uses her skills and talents to be a source of blessing to others.

Sensing the call on her life to preach the gospel of Jesus Christ, Nicole quit her job and immersed herself in her studies at Howard University School of Divinity. During her tenure, she was selected to serve as the Faculty Research Scholar for the esteemed Old Testament Professor, the late Dr. Gene Rice. Nicole was also the recipient of more than $20,000 in scholarships while matriculating at the Divinity School.

Nicole has always spoken her truth and has been a trailblazer in her career. She has served as the first and only African American to serve in her position as an Equal Employment Opportunity/Diversity and Inclusion professional for her organization. She has been the recipient of many awards in this capacity and continues to blaze trails in her industry. She has worked in this area for more than 30 years.

Nicole started her ministry, SISTERGRAM Ministries, in 1998 with a newsletter and a circulation of approximately 125 women in her then local church. In less than two years, the newsletter circulation had grown to more than 2,000 women across the country and in various prisons. Nicole has used her gift of writing to encourage women over the past 20 years. She was honored in October 2018 by the Governor of Maryland for her work with women over the years.

In addition to her writing gift, Nicole held a monthly fellowship for women for 12 years, ministering to more than 1,000 women over that time. She has also hosted a weekly prayer call for the past 15 years and continues to do so today.

Nicole has hosted her own international online show reaching viewers around the world. She also hosted her own radio show on Urban One, formerly Radio One. She is an international best-selling author who wrote four books of her own and served as a contributing writer in more than 40 book projects. She is the recipient of the prestigious 2018 50 Great Writers You Should Be Reading Contest. Her very first anthology, *Faith For Fiery Trials: Testimonies That Will Ignite The Fire In Your Soul And Increase Your Faith In God*, was the 2019 Anthology of the Year presented by the Indie Author Legacy Awards in partnership with Black Enterprise. Nicole was also a finalist for Female Author of the Year and a finalist for the Reader's Choice Award. Her books have been highlighted in several countries: South Africa, South America, Australia, Netherlands, to name a few. She is also a monthly contributing writer in several magazines. Nicole was also selected as the 2019 ACHI Woman of the Year. She was also selected as the

#SpeakerCon Faith-Based Speaker of the Year for 2019.

Nicole is a mentor and a leader's leader, serving as coach and confidante to many high-achieving women in ministry and the marketplace. Women look to her for spiritual guidance and godly wisdom for everyday living. She is an executive leadership coach serving women leaders in the marketplace. She holds a Bachelor of Arts in Sociology from Howard University, a Juris Doctor from the University of the District of Columbia David A. Clarke School of Law, a Master of Law Degree in Litigation and Dispute Resolution from the George Washington University School of Law, and a Master of Divinity from Howard University School of Divinity. She also has a Certificate in Leadership Coaching from Georgetown University and is a certified speaker, trainer, and coach with the John Maxwell Team.

She is an Ambassador for the American Heart Association, turning her pain into purpose. Having lost her mom to heart disease and being diagnosed herself with heart disease shortly after her mother passed away, Nicole has been intentional about spreading the message to other African American women about heart health awareness. Nicole was featured in a commercial sharing her mom's story and her story on more than 12 media outlets in various magazines, newsletters, and jumbotrons at multiple airports.

Nicole completed the Women in Leadership Program at the prestigious Brookings Institute. She also completed the first Women's Leadership Program at her alma mater, George Washington University. Nicole is a professional speaker certified by the National Speakers Association. She is a member of the International Coach Federation, Maryland Bar Association, and the Christian Legal Society.

She currently serves as an Equal Employment Opportunity/Diversity Program Manager at the US Department of Commerce/NOAA Research. She is the recipient of NOAA's highest award for the first Diversity Summit in the Agency's history. She served as a Chapter President and the National Vice President for Compliance for Federally Employed Women(FEW). During her presidency, the chapter was recognized for increasing membership and Community Outreach Projects offering 'Comfy Chemo Bags' to women undergoing chemotherapy and 'Dress For Success,' offering business attire to underprivileged individuals returning to the workforce.

Nicole has spoken at numerous conferences, both sacred and secular, including the Success Women's Conference held in Biloxi, MS, alongside Lisa Nichols and other notable speakers and influencers, Washington Suburban Sanitary Commission (WSSC) Women In Business Conference, American Mothers National Conference, Federally Employed Women's National Training Program, to name a few, making an impact on every platform. She is a world changer destined to help women Show Up Great, Speak Up With Confidence, and Stand Out Courageously!

Other Books And Projects By Nicole S. Mason

Faith For Fiery Trials: Vol III – Triumphant Faith In Trying Times

Faith For Fiery Trials: Men Impacting Men With Real, Raw and Relatable Stories

Faith For Fiery Trials: Vol II – Building Faith One Story At A Time

Faith For Fiery Trials: Testimonies That Will Ignite The Fire In Your Soul And Increase Your Faith In God

Maintain Your Momentum: Success Quotes for High Achieving Women

Monday Morning Motivations: Encouraging Words to Start Your Week

Morning Meditations: Starting Your Day with Passion, Purpose, and Power

Meditaciones Matinales: Comenzando Tu Dia Con Proposito Pasión Y Poder

Contributing Author In The Following Books

Chicken Soup for the Soul®: Miracles & Divine Intervention – 101 Stories of Faith and Hope
Presented By Amy Newmark

Glambitious Guide to Faith, Self-Care & Happiness
An Ebook Presented by Glam Boss Organization

Girl, Get Up & Win Everyday: Daily Inspiration and Stories that Motivate You to Go!
Compiled By Telishia Berry
Publisher of Courageous Woman Magazine

Hope Renewed: Transformational Messages of Hope, Healing &
Inspiration To Renew Your Spirit
Presented By Dr. Cheryl Wood and 100 global speakers

She Is Well: Stories of Power, Strength, Wellness
Presented By Delayna Watkins

You Are Enough! Messages of Inspiration & Empowerment To Live
Your Best Life
Presented By Les Brown And Dr. Cheryl Wood

Live Your Faith Out Loud: Real-life Stories Compelling You to do
More!
Presented By Dorothy Patrick Wilson

I Am A Victor!: Stories of Individuals Who Victoriously Turned
Their Pain Into Purpose
Presented By Dr. Cheryl Wood

The Unstoppable Warrior Woman: Inspirational Stories of Women
Who Overcame the Odds and Chose to Thrive
Presented By Bershan Shaw

Glambitious Guide To Win in 2021
An Ebook Presented By Glam Boss Organization

Speaking My Truth: 50 Real Life Stories That Inspire, Empower,
Heal and Transform
Presented By Cheryl Wood

Beyond Inspiration: 14 Transformational Prayers To Increase Your
Impact and Influence Presented By Melissa J. Nixon

Daily Dose of Declarations: A 365-Day Journey To Help You
Declare Positive Affirmations Over Your Life
Presented By Melanie Bonita

The Breaking To Brilliance: 15 Powerful Stories Of Triumph and Healing
Presented By Dr. Valeka Moore

No More Chains – It's Time For Change: 11 Real Life Transformations Empowering You To Release Mental, Emotional, and Generational Chains
Presented By Ari Squires

Letters to My Legacy Volume 1: Letters of Love From a Mother's Heart
Compiled by Rhonda Watts Robinson

Voices of the 21st Century: Women Who Influence, Inspire and Make a Difference
Presented by Nicole S. Mason and Gail Watson

Glambitious Guide To Win in 2019
An Ebook Presented By Glam Boss Organization

Push Through: How The Process Leads To The Promise
An Ebook Presented By Glam Boss Organization

I Am Healed: Healing Devotional Anthology
Compiled By Rhonda Watts Robinson

What Is A Courageous Woman: A Collaborative Book Featuring 78 Co-Authors Celebrating Courageous Women
Presented By Telishia Berry
Publisher of Courageous Woman Magazine

Glambitious Guide To Greatness: How To Go From Doubt To Destiny & From Surviving To Thriving
An E-book Presented By Glam Boss Organization

Behind The Scenes of a Phenomenal Woman: Featuring Stories of 24 Phenomenal Women Presented By Dr. Chantelle Teasdell

Women Inspiring Nations: 25 Women Sharing Their Stories and Gifts to Inspire and Transform Lives Across Nations
Presented By Cheryl Wood

Igniting the Fire: A Woman's Guide to Setting a Blaze in Ministry, Business, and Life
Presented By LaTracey Copeland Hughes

The Fearless Living Experience: Bold and Empowered Women Share Their Triumph Over Life's Curveballs
Presented By Cheryl Wood

Made in the USA
Middletown, DE
14 October 2023

40660144R00091